Awakening Memories

also by H.T.A. Heisler

doctor ken
*a true story about a man
and the
Hippocratic Oath*

written as Creative Nonfiction
story told by H.T.A. Heisler
with writings by
Kehnroth Schramm, M.D.

* * *

Packets of Seeds
*Messages from Kehnroth Schramm, M.D.
describing Life After Passing*

(Compiled and Edited by H.T.A. Heisler)

* * *

The Innkeeper's Daughter
A Christmas Story and Music Score

Christmas carol and lullaby music score
for
voices, piano, guitars

(Not designed for small children.)
This book has full color pages.
Four pages of music composition for musicians.

Awakening Memories

short stories
H.T.A. Heisler

ISBN 978-0-9917756-6-8 Printed book
ISBN 978-0-9917756-7-5 Ebook

dedication

To a Wild Rose
Wherever you are and
whatever happens in your life,
remember,
someone, somewhere
loves and appreciates you
unconditionally and freely
... forever ...

TABLE OF CONTENTS

Table of Contents continued

Table of Contents continued

INTRODUCTION

The stories in this book are based on true experiences with cosmic energy, insight, and awakening memories. The stories are not intended to be about me or any other person; instead, the stories are intended to encourage thought and conversation about the extraordinary and paranormal that affect each and every one of us all the time. As a writer, I wish to free people who are keeping their experiences secret.

Painted with words like a Chagall painting, these stories live in the fabric of the universe and are told in this story circle where there is no up, no down, no beginning and no ending.

H. T. A. Heisler

Just another Story

THE LIFE OF A MANUSCRIPT

Summers in the prairie city of Regina can be hot and dry. As a young girl, I spent my summers at the swimming pool right next to Dewdney Avenue where the tiny hut that jailed Louis Riel still stood. Beside it was the white Grace Haven building where unwed pregnant girls and women were hidden from society until their babies were born and taken from them.

In the circle of swimming and diving and getting cold in the water, I would lay on the cement around the pool to warm up in the sunshine. That is where I spent hours of every summer, taking in what was right in front of me. There were extremes of life to think about in those buildings. Birth happened on one side, coupled with heartbreak and loss; death happened on the other side, coupled with heartbreak and loss.

My gaze would often start at the prominent white building. Though Grace Haven was silent on the outside, I felt that I could hear the cries of desperate women and babies lost to each other inside the building. It seemed unbearable even to think about.

My attention would stay with the weathered grey hut. It was hard to imagine any human being living there from May to the middle of November. The intense sun of summer would bake a person in that tiny space and the months of September to November can be freezing. I imagined that Riel was living in a confined hell on earth.

Rumors were all I had. I understood that Riel was a hero to some and a traitor to others. The man captured my interest day after day, year after year. In my youth, I was filled with curiosity about the man and I found myself admiring the hero.

Growing up on the prairies, I easily took Riel's side in any disagreement he may have had with the Canadian government run by men of eastern provinces. I could not imagine those strangers having any understanding of prairie people, especially of the Indians or those who were Métis. Many of my own family were immigrant farmers and those government officials always appeared uptight and loud-mouthed, opposite of soft-spoken people I knew. I understood the Riel who fought to protect homelands of Métis people on the prairies. I looked out across the prairies and felt Riel's struggle as though he was in the air around me.

My quest to really know him took form in my twenties. As a mother of small children and working full time for the Saskatchewan government, I had little spare time. In my hour-long lunch break,

I would make a beeline to the main public library and use a half hour to research the life and times of Riel. With my handwritten notes, I would head back to the Legislative Building.

Evenings after my children were in bed and the chores done, I would sort notes and write.

A statue of a naked Louis Riel had been erected on the lawn of the Saskatchewan Legislative Building. The sculptor, John Nugent, was chastised for the naked monument and forced to cover Riel. He put a bronze cape around Riel. People lined up to look under the cape at Riel's bare genitals while I was looking into the bare facts of his life in library records.

Someone challenged me to look. Not really believing that he was naked, I took a turn, bent down, peered up, and turned away. I felt Riel's humiliation.

In time, I wrote a large manuscript intended for a book about Louis Riel. Then life took a sudden turn. When I confronted my husband about on-going adultery, he promised to leave his adulterous behavior behind if I would run away with him and the children.

We were leaving Regina to make a new start. The manuscript and accompanying notes were packed along with minimal belongings into a box on top of an old car to spend the summer on the road, passing though the Red River country where Riel was born, stopping along the way at various camping spots and small cottages until at the end of summer, we reached Toronto.

The manuscript moved into a nice house in Toronto. During this time, we met a Buddhist monk and a group of people who were searching for something new and different, maybe even enlightenment. Together, we founded a meditation centre in the lake country.

My family moved into the log cabin on four hundred acres of forested land. I carried the manuscript to its new home on the second floor of the cabin where we slept. For several months I was the cook and the caretaker as crowds of people came and went.

One morning, I watched my husband walk out the door into the freezing winter day of January. As the door was closing behind his red plaid jacket, I intuitively knew he was not coming back. He had continued his adulterous ways in the tents of women on the meditation centre. He had again been found out. Without a word, even though I was pregnant, he chose to leave the children and me on the meditation centre while he took off for bright lights of Toronto where he continued conquering more women.

A monk stayed on to help me out in the midst of winter in a place that had no modern conveniences. He stayed in another small cabin but took care of providing wood for the stoves in my house, and entertained the children with Sanskrit writing lessons. I took care of his meals and we often kept each other company by the warmth of the stove in the evening.

One night the monk built a giant bonfire outside. Dressed only in his saffron robe and big winter boots, he was burning old wood from cages that had been left by previous owners who ran a mink farm. The bonfire circle was about ten feet high and several feet wide in the midst of a field of white snow. Sparks of fire were flying high against the black sky sprinkled with millions of twinkling stars. It was a spectacular scene. He explained that it was a cleansing fire and asked if I had anything I wanted to throw in.

With snow on my boots, I ran up the wooden staircase to my bedroom. In haste, I gathered an armful of clothing and the paper box that held the manuscript and reams of notes. I ran outside with parts of my life.

One swoosh and I threw them all into the fire. With cold snow under my feet and the heat of fire on my face, I watched writing on papers catch brilliant flames that slowly shrunk the papers and curled them into charcoal, releasing into smoke all the ideas and hard work of months.

After all those years of possessing him, I was letting Riel go as I stood there feeling release in the night air. Somehow I was giving him freedom.

Should I consider this my failure, perhaps a waste of time? I would regret a moment of madness when I burned my clothes, especially the pretty, flowered, mauve, rayon crepe dress my mother had sewn for me years ago, and a broach of three intertwined rings that my mother had given to me, which must have been attached to an item landing in the fire. I would remember my mother whenever I thought about that night. My mother's smiling face and the whirling sound of her Singer treadle sewing machine as she sewed the dresses for me were more important than any manuscript.

What I had written was a document that repeated information kept in the library. By research, I had come to know Louis Riel's bravery, determination, intelligence, and his self-sacrifice for people. I found him to be a writer. During his time in jail, he wrote poetry, and he wrote about high morals that I read as prayers from a man filled with love. I had been right in my admiration of a man who eventually became recognized as a leader and politician who brought Manitoba into Confederation by forming a provisional government and presenting Canada with a Bill of Rights. Though he was found guilty and hanged for treason, time has rescued the reputation of Louis Riel, now known as a martyr and as the Father of Manitoba.

I was born too late to know the man in his lifetime, and through historical papers, it was impossible to know the man as I wanted to know him. I was unable to write the creative nonfiction book that I wanted to write with true understanding. I had not the right experiences yet in my own young life to write the life of a man like Louis David Riel.

I never regretted burning the manuscript; it had its life and gave it up in a blaze of glory when the time was right. I considered the burning of the manuscript to be growth in my own journey to learn the art of writing.

Just another Story

A TRUE STORY

Many of my stories come to me on the waterfront. Always preferring to be outdoors, as usual between Pacific storms, I was watching the salt-water retreat in an extraordinary low tide. Small boats and cargo ships traveled to their destinations. Seaplanes took off and landed. Amid the activity, the heads of harbor seals would pop up and disappear again. Geese and seagulls flew overhead. It was noisy with all the activity and at the same time it was quiet; time to relax in the outdoors and think.

In that scene, I was remembering an event that is the story I want to tell you, my reader, as the introduction to this book, Awakening Memories. It is a true story.

I had boarded a train in Ontario with my children in search of a new start in life and found it at the end of earth on the west coast. Kitsilano in Vancouver was my home at the time of this story.

I was a young single parent with five children aged ten to a few months – the youngest being born premature a couple of days after arriving.

I was used to people dropping in on me because I had been living in a meditation centre where it had been my job to look after everyone who came and went. I was the caretaker of many people's daily needs and I cooked their meals. People followed me for reasons unknown to me. They came in great number to my door, some from Ontario, some from Saskatchewan, and some from up and down the west coast as they heard about me. Some found me for reasons of their own, like the men from my prairie hometown, who put a giant fishing boat in my backyard to renovate. Being new to the west coast, I reasoned that at least I had a boat to float in case of natural disaster. Determined men arrived with various proposals. Some people thought I had something to teach. I thought I had nothing to teach, but they kept coming anyway. I would feed them and play my guitar for them, even give them a safe place to sleep if they came from a great distance, just not with me, and then I would send them on their way.

One afternoon, a woman stood in my open doorway. She was a black woman, tall and slender. Her long multicolored dress swaddled her body and she wore a multicolored turban on her head. She was the most exotic person I had even seen.

"I've come to cook dinner for you," she said.

I did not question why or how come or where she came from or who sent her. As I said, I was so used to people of all sorts coming to my door, that it never occurred to me that this was odd. When I think back, my children were living in my world and this was their world along with me.

Under her arm, she had a small bag of groceries. We went into the kitchen and started cooking like we were best friends. She did tell me she was from Nigeria in Africa.

As we cooked, she told me stories. One story has stood out in my memory all these years later and this is the story that started this book.

> *An American woman was traveling Africa with her husband. When they came to a small village, the woman saw a man with many wives. Meeting with him, she experienced awakened memories. In a former life, she and the man had been husband and wife, and had loved each other deeply. Now, she could not bear to leave him again. She sent her American husband home without her. She gave up the luxury of her American life to stay in a village that had none of the modern conveniences she had been used to.*
>
> *She stayed with the African man as his wife in that small village even though he had other wives. She became his favorite wife.*

When the dinner was cooked, the woman walked out of the house and disappeared. I never saw her again.

The story she told had me thinking about why people are attracted together with no boundaries, seemingly odd to others living in the definition of time. That question first came to my attention when I was twelve years old. My girlfriend and I babysat two little boys whose parents seemed to us to be mismatched. To our young minds, the wife was not at all good looking and she was old compared to her young, very handsome husband who was so completely in love with his wife that my girlfriend and I forgot to have a crush on him. Instead, we had lively debates about the question of why. We never did solve the question then.

People love and come together in odd kinds of pairing. Age, beauty, color are transcended when we have awakened memories. We can experience the timeless zone, a dimensionless place where we love and want to be with a loved one from a distant past, a place not obvious to others.

Just another Story

JUST CUPS

In a Greek Myth, Hebe, daughter of Zeus and Hera, was a Cupbearer and Goddess of eternal youth. Hebe served nectar and ambrosia to the gods and goddesses of Mount Olympus from a cup.

Ambrosia

In myth Ambrosia, the drink of the Gods, was brought from earth by doves to the gods in Olympus. Ambrosia is supposed to bestow immortality on anyone who consumes it. Honey is supposed to be a source of Ambrosia.

Cups – Goblet – footed cup – or Chalice, which is Latin borrowed from Greek. The cup is used in Mass for sipping wine that represents the blood of Christ. Jesus used a cup that became known as the Holy Grail at the Last Supper with bread. This was the beginning of communion as known in the Catholic and Anglican Churches.

two cups

I was just turning thirty and starting over as a single parent. I was happy within myself, relishing in finding myself after a large part of me had been given away and maybe even lost. I was whole again!

I was still a young, healthy, vibrant female, joyful about everything in my life. I especially felt looked after by some cosmic source or guardian angels from the source of creative energy. It especially had been shown to me when we arrived in a new city and within a couple of days, my baby was born premature. I was told she might not live but she did and was healthy. I believed my children were gifts from the vibrant source of life.

Several months later, I opened my eyes in the morning. Coming out of a deep sleep, I was now in the place between sleeping and waking. In a vision right in front of my open eyes were two cups side by side in the air. The cups were simple in shape, brown in color, but on closer look they were not simple, they were purposely significant; one was a smaller female cup, the other was clearly a larger male cup.

I watched as the two cups slowly moved closer together. The cups touched each other and merged. At the merging of the two cups, the female and male within my own body fused in intense energy and blissful ecstasy.

Then I was wide-awake, lying on my back in bed with the breeze of morning air touching me through the open window. Nothing like it had ever happened before. The aftermath was of satisfaction, extreme surprise and puzzlement as to why this had happened. Was I being taught something about how we are complete within ourselves?

I wondered about spirit, having heard that spirits can take on different genders through incarnations; but I was not concerned with spirit this time. I emerged with new knowledge of what it means to be human. Always thinking of myself as completely female and never desiring to be anything other than female, I understood for the first time how human bodies do have both genders, one being predominant from conception.

This experience turned my attention to the meaning and power of cups. Why were cups brought to me – to show what humans are capable of?

a paper cup

My own first significant experience with a cup was when I was five years old. My family had just moved to a new house. It was a hot summer day and I was eager to find friends in a new neighborhood. I wandered onto the street. Following the sounds of young voices, I bravely entered a yard and followed a narrow walkway to round the house. In the back yard four girls, all a few years older than me, were on a porch just a few steps off the ground. I stood there, looking up. They spotted me.

"Come on up."

I walked up the few stairs and did not say anything. Instead I waited, noticing that all the girls were holding little white cups.

"Here, have a drink."

The tallest girl poured water from a jug into another white cup and handed it to me. I took the cup and was horrified as it bent together and water spilled over my foot onto the porch.

"You broke the cup. Get lost!" The girl yelled.

I backed away with the paper cup in my hand. Dropping it, I ran. I had never held a paper cup before and had never been so humiliated by people.

The experience of that cup would stay with me for the rest of my life. When I would see people being humiliated for one reason or another, I would often refer back to feelings of that day, and how it set up a lifelong instinct to look after the underdog.

ceremonial cups

During my young years, I noticed that cups or vessels for drinking were used in symbolic ways. At the wedding of my uncle, a glass was wrapped in a white napkin and put on the floor in the middle of all the people. My father, looking dapper in his suit and white shirt, stomped the bundle with his right foot to break the glass, and joyfully yelled something to everyone. I wondered what breaking the glass meant. I made up my own meaning that it was symbolic of breaking the old and good luck in a new beginning. Only in years later, did that scene raise more questions since my family was not known to be Jewish.

At first communion, I was presented with a sip of wine from a chalice that was wiped with a white napkin between kids and turned a small turn for the next kid to sip. I was told we were taking in the blood of Christ. I thought that was a stomach churning idea and chose not to think of it that way; instead, I enjoyed the fruity flavor but wondered about germs since I was a finicky eater, always watching out for cleanliness and refusing to eat if I suspected any dirt. For me to accept communion in this way was a stretch. I could not disappoint my mother who had sewn a beautiful white dress for me to wear on this occasion, and she was watching in anticipation of my soul being – what? – I had no idea even though I had attended all the classes that were supposed to teach me what. I felt young and immortal just as I was before and after communion.

the gift

Over the years, cups had been given to me as gifts. On my thirtieth birthday, my young son had saved his money to buy an ornamental vase for me. It had sculpted figures around the outside under painted plaster in the shape of a footed chalice. I sat on the steps to my front porch on this summer night when an abundance of shooting stars danced across the turquoise sky. The vase felt magical as I held it on my lap. I pretended that some of the stars were landing in my vase as good luck for my birthday and starting over again.

Men had been checking me out regularly. I was amazed at the number of men, especially the men just nineteen and twenty years old, who were interested in a woman with five children. Not only were the young men interested, but a couple of them tried hard to convince me that sexually our compatibility was better because of our age difference. It was humorous to me. I was fine by myself for now.

On the evening of my birthday, a well-known journalist and environmental activist showed up out of the blue as I was sitting on the staircase with my cup and looking at the stars. I had known of him but my only interest in him was about his work. He sat beside me for a couple of hours, trying to have a normal conversation as I held the vase and watched for shooting stars. He never returned. I was okay with that; after all I had shown little interest in him that evening.

Many of the special cups given to me, have sat out in the open on tables and desks, holding treasures of pens, pencils and brushes for writing and artwork. I am always excited at what fascinating ideas pour out of those powerful tools.

the cup

clean your cup

For years, my ex-husband had been flaunting his lovers in my face and telling me that I was not as highly evolved as he and his friends because I would not sleep around like they were. So when I moved away, years later he telephoned because he had traveled across the country to see me. He had never asked about the children in the past, nor had he offered even a little support. All I ever wanted was for him to ask how they were. When he still did not ask about the children, I told him, "Get lost!"

He angrily yelled at me through the telephone, "Clean your cup!"

His words, "Clean your cup!" rattled in my brain for a long time afterward. And every time I remembered those words, I thought, "How dare he!"

Zen meditation

At the invitation of my Japanese friend, I attended a Zen meditation session at the Buddhist Centre. He chose to sit us in the centre of rows of people who all immediately went into meditation. I crossed my legs and closed my eyes.

Suddenly I heard a crack that sounded, for the life of me, like someone being hit. I peeked. Sure enough, two robed men were wandering around the room with long sticks cracking meditators over their shoulders. Panic struck me. Fear overcame any desire I may have had to be in the room and meditate. Endurance became the task. Somehow I had to remain seated and not run out of the room, displaying my fear. In what seemed like hours later but turned out to be an hour, it was over.

My friend invited me for the tea ceremony that followed meditation. I was curious. Not ever having attended the ceremony before, I did not know what to expect. Shoeless, we made our way into a small room with cushions on the floor beside low tables. Surprised to find myself one of only a small group now, I felt uneasy. It was too easy to do something wrong. I had read that the tea ceremony is also a meditation; you meditate on the tea and speak only pleasantries.

The Meditation Master came in and took his place. Tiptoeing Japanese girls with big smiles served the tea in tiny cups. There were long silences as we sipped tea. I noted the color, the taste, the feel on my lips, tongue and followed it to my stomach. I noted the feel of the cup, the look of the cup, all the time being aware of the silence totally filling the room; it was a noisy silence.

After the tea was drunk, the Master spoke a few pleasantries and some Zen thought.

Later, I told my friend that I had been frightened of the men with the sticks and could not relax.

"That's the idea. You're not supposed to relax and get lazy. The sticks are to keep you awake so you won't miss anything in meditation by falling asleep. But they don't hit you until you've been here three times. You were safe."

My friend invited me to attend again but I declined. The thought of those sticks was not enticing to my way of thinking.

cup of healing

Cups are used as measurements of achievement in awards. They are also used to show acknowledgement. When I had been meditating and moving the kundalini energy upward from chakra to chakra, it suddenly got stuck in my throat and would not move higher. It felt like a flame was in my throat, waving around. My throat was on fire with laryngitis.

Three days later, I rushed to see my meditation teacher. He listened, then, he left the room. I sat alone for a few minutes just waiting for something to happen.

He came back with a cup in his hand. This cup would be his vessel of healing.

He was a man of great height now standing over me as he handed the cup to me and said, "Drink."

I felt small under his height. Taking the cup filled with a steaming creamy looking broth, I said, "It's too hot!"

"Drink."

"But it's too hot!" Thinking about the three bears story, I wanted to laugh.

"Drink." He looked serious.

I drank and burned my mouth.

"You have karma in your throat."

He looked pleased.

After three days, my throat felt normal. In meditation, I managed to move the energy up through my throat. Of course, I did have to wonder about what karma I had carried in my throat. Asking to know in a dream, I found a clue but could not verify it since it apparently was from another incarnation. True or not, it was enough to convince me to closely watch my words from then on ... then I forgot.

the carnelian stone

I had packed my children onto a train to travel four days across the country to some unknown place. I did not know what I would find there or how we would survive. At the end of train tracks, I found and rented a house by the sea that was designated for demolition in future. For now, I was grateful to have a whole house for my children.

Outside the living room window, a large tree was in full bloom with an abundance of fragrant white flowers. Someone said they were Orange blossoms but never grew oranges. I did not really know what they were but the flowers seemed like a gift from the universe and were part of my daily enjoyment of life. Every day, I would reach through the open window and take a fresh flower to wear just over my ear in my long, golden-brown hair. I would enjoy the fragrance for hours. Just as I had placed the flower in my hair this day, there was a knock on the door.

A young man, who had become a friend while I lived on the meditation centre, was traveling with his friend and stopped by to visit as many old friends continued to do. They had come thousands of miles. As usual, I opened my home to traveling friends, so they settled in for a few days. My children and I slept in the private upstairs bedrooms, while the living room was open for people to roll out their sleeping bags for nights they stayed. I did not have any real furniture after leaving all my furniture behind just a few months ago, so I had fashioned many colorful, large cushions around a large, old, Persian rug that I found at the Salvation Army Thrift Store and bought for three dollars, and it even came with an under-pad. I always felt the salesman gave it to me because it was worth more than three dollars. Not only that, but years later I would find a picture of the rug in a book because it was rare, special and worth a small fortune.

It was quite a comfortable room. People liked to lounge in it. I had found a ten-dollar guitar in a corner store and hung on the wall. No matter what else was going on in the room, I would pick the guitar up and play softly. Whenever I reached a goal in playing a desired piece of music, the phrase would run through my head that 'the more you know, the more you know you don't know', because there was always another and harder piece of music to learn. Life felt soft and good with my music.

On arrival, my friend handed an orange carnelian stone to me with the words, "Now your true love will come to you."

I thought that was a kind wish to give me.

I had never seen a carnelian before. I thought it so beautiful that I went immediately to the wise old man in the Persian Arts Shop. I had discovered him in my exploration of my new city. He charmed me with his knowledge. As I watched him do business, he taught me how to give away time. No matter how busy his shop was, he gave each person all the time needed with him. I always waited. I received time and good feelings in each visit. He introduced me to the tiny vials of wild rose perfume that I now wore.

I wondered about the properties of the stone. The Persian man explained that carnelian is believed to hold warm energy that is connected to sexuality, fertility and the root chakra. I asked him to set it in a ring.

The next day, I was wearing the ring and proudly admiring it, but not connecting it to my houseguests even though I was becoming aware of sexual vibrations from both men.

I still did not connect the giver's wish to the gift.

One night, my friend made his way into my bedroom in high hopes, only to be asked to leave. He was nice about it and did leave.

That same night, I had a dream of the kind that is more than just a dream – it was a lucid dream that when awake, carried clarity of reality. A woman came to me in the dream, warning me that downstairs the friend of my friend was practicing a magical routine that he hoped would bring me to him sexually. The woman told me that I was being warned so that I would not fall under his command. I asked the woman in the dream, what would happen if I did give in. The woman was adamant, "Do not be tempted. The man is not right for you."

In the morning, my friend greeted me. After his failure, jealousy was now bothering him. He was convinced his friend would win me.

He explained, "My friend thinks he is in love with you. But you should know that he is trying to seduce you with magic. He stays awake in the night. He makes a circle on the living room rug and walks in the circle doing some sort of ceremony that is suppose to make you love him and have sex with him. He has also started to wander around in the daytime, calling your name under his breath. I think you should be aware of this."

While my children and I were asleep upstairs, unaware of what was going on, the man had been practicing magic of sorts every night. Rather than enter my bedroom, he had a different tactic in mind. The living room became his domain at night. He would wear his special cap, make imaginary circles on my Persian rug and practice his magical rites, chanting my name continually.

I was not only surprised, but I felt violated. I shuddered. In no way was I attracted to the man who was determined to seduce me. I was determined to be careful and watchful.

I started chanting a mantra for strength. I chanted my favorite mantra, Om Mani Padme Hum, over and over. I had used this mantra silently through many of life's difficult situations – through labor and giving birth – through my baby's illness and hospitalization where an intuitive doctor in Emergency asked the nurse if the mother could speak English even though I had not uttered a word out loud in any language in his vicinity. The mantra had always given me energy and strength. Now, no matter what I was doing, I was also chanting in the back of my mind.

I knew he was still trying, too, because when I would leave the house for a while, from down the street I could see him out on the street in front of the house waiting and watching for me. I would be pushing my baby carriage, looking like a normal mother on the outside, but looking over to the mountains and gaining strength while chanting into the clear air of the mountains. I could still see him but I felt strong.

I did not have long to wait for something to happen. One afternoon, I was sitting on a cushion in the living room and playing my guitar. Across the room, my friend was having a casual conversation with another person who had dropped in to visit. Magic man walked into the room with two heavy white coffee mugs from the kitchen – one in each hand held out in front of his chest. He came directly toward me and knelt down in front of me. He set the cups on the rug in front of me. I could see they were half filled with cooking oil.

I laid my guitar down beside me and watched with interest. People in the room went still and silent as they watched.

Slowly, he lit a fire in each cup and brought his hands together over the two fires. He then picked up the cups and held them, one in each hand in front of me at my eye level.

Instinctively, I knew what they meant: I was one fire and he was the other. It dawned on me that I had been given a lesson about the meaning of these cups in that sexual lucid dream before this day. I knew that his intention was to draw the two flames together into one flame and that was to draw me to him in a sexual union.

He was concentrating hard while looking at me with intensity as he slowly started moving the cups together.

It was now a battle of wills. I tried hard to maintain a serene, calm exterior while mentally I was in a battle of my lifetime. My whole future depended on this moment. Using all my mental strength, I was determined that the flames would not become one. I concentrated on the cups to keep them apart.

The battle was on.

He was physically trying so hard to bring the cups together that his hands were turning white. Veins stood out in his arms. He was so intense that his face was stiff in a grimace. The flames were in his eyes.

Lasting a few minutes, I could feel the pressure coming from him. I fought back, determined to hold the cups apart.

Suddenly, there was a loud bang. The two cups that were close, but not yet touching, exploded in mid air. Two separate flames of fire flew upward and extinguished in the air. The oil spilled to the floor. He held two broken cups in his hands. He looked shocked. He lost. He slumped back on his heals in defeat.

I leaned back against the wall. I won!

He and I exchanged no words and no one in the room commented. There was only silence as he picked himself up and left the room looking dejected and shocked.

The next day, the men picked up their bags and left. They would never return. The battle of wills over cups, magic circles, fire, and seduction was over.

As they drove away, I went to the open window and plucked a blossom from the Orange tree. Holding the white Orange flower and still wearing the ring with the orange carnelian because it felt nice, I stopped to admire it. I sent up a wish that one day my true, beloved lover would find me. I placed the flower in my hair over my ear. I would enjoy the fragrance of the flower's nectar and my freedom in the new day.

Just another Story

FIGHT OR FLIGHT

Her husband would come home drunk after spending his income on parties and gambling. His blue eyes looked black as he would be physically violent toward her. Recently, he was also threatening violence to their small children. The last time he came home drunk, he entered the children's bedroom as they lay sleeping, but she had persuaded him to follow her out of the room.

She lay in bed listening to the unfettered prairie wind howl around the corners of the small house. The children were asleep, two small boys in the bedroom across the hall, and baby girl in a crib in her mother's room. The wind was peaceful because it was a sound she was used to. At the same time, the howl was jangling her senses, knowing that violence might be coming through the door at any moment. She was on wait, watch and listen.

It spread across her like a shadow of doom; knowing that if he were to be violent toward the children, she would defend them in whatever violent manner was necessary and possible, just to end it. Violence toward her was one thing but her instinctive, motherly protection of her children was a different matter. She realized that his life might be in danger.

Thinking through scenarios, she questioned what she had on hand to defend her children? He was much larger and stronger than she, so her hands and feet would never be a match to his drunken strength. She could only think of a knife from the kitchen, which was all she had. That scared her. She hated blood. Just the thought of harming him or any living mammal was a horrible idea.

Fight or flight. She had to decide. As she lay in bed, surrounded by darkness and howling wind that seemed to be especially loud tonight, she knew that if she stayed in this marriage, she would end up brain damaged because he had already put her head through a plaster wall, crushing her skull, and he had scarred her face more than once. He had pulled out a gun and threatened to shoot her if she left him. She knew that life just could not go on with a deadly result of either her or him, or worse – the children. If the children lived without physical injury, what would the long-term emotional damage be because of living with this, year after year?

She thought about all the help she had sought. She had looked for counseling from the church minister who had married them. The minister said her husband had a right to his family on his terms and that he, the minister, would beat her, too. That admission from the minister scared her so much she would never consider going near him or his church again.

She had tried calling the police and was told they did not interfere in family matters. The one time the police did come to the house was when she had called from a neighbor's house. When she entered the house with the police, her husband was sitting with the children as though he was an angel. The police left immediately. The other time she talked to the police was when she had open wounds and fresh blood all over her swollen face and the police told her she had to press charges for them to do anything. Pressing charges might send him to jail. She decided not to do that because she felt sorry for him. She wanted someone to stop him but she did not want to hurt him.

She had only her parents and they harbored her and her children whenever she turned up but were powerless otherwise. In fact, her husband had lied to her parents and blamed her for his problems. She would leave her parents' home just to keep the peace for them.

Taking flight ... leaving on her own steam was her only option, but she had left him before and he had tracked her down through his friends who followed her to and from work. He then broke the door down to the second floor apartment she had rented. Ironically, in that situation, she and the children were all cowering on one bed and the bed crashed to the floor at the same second that he crashed through the door. Somehow, he had bypassed the distraught landlady who had followed him upstairs and stood watching from behind him. The landlady was glad to see her leave immediately with the children.

This time, leaving would have to be foolproof. She had to go to work in the morning because she was in fact the sole income earner to pay rent for the house, to feed her children and pay for their daycare. His income was always spent on gambling, women and drunken parties in hotel rooms. She decided to act normally when he would come home tonight and tomorrow she would lay plans to leave … but how?

That night when he did come home, he was drunk, loud and violent. His eyes were dark with a horror going on deep within himself. He grabbed at her. She dodged and ran until she led him out of the house and away from the children. In pajamas and bare feet, she ended up in her vegetable garden. The garden was in a corner of the yard under a street lamp and by a bus stop. Now that they were out in the open and neighbors could hear, he seemed to calm down and wobbled into the house. She panicked and followed to find him collapsed on the sofa in the living room, now sleeping it off.

While he was at work one day soon after that night, she cleared out. She took her children to another city to start over. Out of fear that he would come after her, she changed her name so that no one could trace her unless she wanted contact.

He came home to an empty house. Guilt at leaving the way she did and taking children away from a father would follow her but she balanced guilt with the belief that she saved her children and possibly her own life. She would pray for his wellbeing. She knew she had never really loved him; any notion of that had been rubbed out before it really started, but she cared about him.

She and the children stayed hidden but she watched her back all the time.

In months to follow, a new friend – a short, roly-poly, sixty-five year old woman, who looked like a white-haired pixy, became a guest in her home, staying for several months. She was in fact, a nun.

Over dinner, the older woman often spoke of her life experiences and gave advice subtly with her stories to the young mother still in her mid-twenties and eager to learn.

This day, the nun was showing the younger woman how she made chicken soup. She boiled the chicken in a large pot of water with a bit of salt. When done, she shredded the chicken meat back into the broth and discarded the bones and skin. Then she shredded fresh, green lettuce into the chicken pot. That was it. In a bowl, soy sauce and hot sauce could be added to taste. It was that simple.

As they sat around the table after eating the chicken soup and the children had left the table, the older woman told another story.

"I was once consumed with jealousy, enough to consider killing someone. I was standing on a cliff. Below me were two important people in my life. One was a woman friend just a little younger than myself. The other was a Buddhist monk who I had grown very fond of. They were walking together on the beach below me. I picked up the biggest rock I could manage with my two hands and held it over the cliff. I was going to drop it on his head. Why him rather than her is because if I killed him, she could not have his company. If I killed her, he would not be my friend. As I stood there holding the rock high in the air, I came to my senses and realized that killing was simply a moment of madness. I would instead have to deal with the war within me – my jealousy. We all have the instinct within us to defend our ideas, our bodies, our egos, our lives, and our loved ones. We have the instinct to fight or take flight. What we do with those basic instincts makes the difference."

"Oh, I could never have the instinct to kill," the younger woman said.

There was a minute of silence while the older woman allowed the thought to churn in the younger woman.

She had been looking down, deep in thought and looked up with a startling realization. "Actually, I did come to the point of having to make a decision of fight or flight. I had to leave my husband because I knew I would have to fight, even to the death of one of us, if I stayed. I could no longer allow him to beat me or the children."

"Yes, you made a decision on one of the basics of life."

"I feel bad because he was a tortured soul. He always claimed he loved me."

The nun asked, "What is love? Is love wanting to hurt and maybe destroy the person you love?"

The younger woman responded, "No. Of course not."

The nun explained, "The word Love is referred to in many ways with underlying meanings – the desire for possession – control – sex – romance. Possession means ownership. Control is a form of possession and exercising power. Sex is a basic animal instinct and can be had without love. Romance can be a mixture of fantasy, memory, and hero worship, and can be used to enhance a situation for sex, control, and possession. Romance has its own power and can lead to love. Love – pure love is unconditional. Love is without boundary. Love is intangible but when you love, you only want the best for the person you love. Love is infinite. When we have children, we learn how to love unconditionally. Love is so basic that animals love unconditionally. For example, we see that kind of unconditional love in dogs and horses. We often get mixed up about what is love."

"I never really thought about it in this way...."

The younger woman had a lot to think about. Then she asked, "What about those people who seem to have love at first sight? I have met a guy recently who said he saw his wife walking. He only saw the back of her and knew he was seeing his wife. They are married now."

"Yes, and the question arises: Where was he before he was born? There was some memory of a relationship with his wife that comes from a life greater than his life on earth. It is not like he fell in love with her while meeting her and getting to know her. Instead, he knew her without even seeing her face. There was an invisible bond already in place that he recognized."

"It is so romantic."

The face of wisdom framed by fluffy white hair, smiled, "Yes, it is."

Just another Story

WORM HOLES

Letter to a Sister

You asked the question, "Why don't dead people just go where they are supposed to go and stop hanging around?"

I need to write you a letter because in our conversations, thoughts get lost. We humans have an audit system that is strong. Writing can be re-read. Let me ask a few questions before I explain what I do know.

Where are dead people to go? Are they supposed to be sent to a distant place that is like people going to another country, never to come back? Where is that place in space? Are they to go to another planet or disappear into nothingness?

Who is invading whom? Are dead people in our space or are we in theirs?

How come we accept angels in our space but cannot accept souls that look like our dead relatives?

Scientists have great fun exploring the term "wormhole" because they play with what one can do within a wormhole. They ponder a tunnel connecting two things, two worlds, where they imagine time travel back and forth can be done. Most often, the wormhole is deliberated in connection with gravity and Einstein's theory of relativity, which is a simple way to predict everything. Scientists discuss two types of wormholes even though they have apparently never proven either one exists.

Worm Holes, or portals are terms some science fiction writers might use to explain the way we have access into an alternate universe and time travel into history or into the future.

A more common term used by people accessing the spirit world is the veil. We imagine a curtain hung between our worlds. We can peek or glimpse through a curtain moved aside or one that is too flimsy to keep us out temporarily. We can peak into life beyond death but usually we have only a limited view and limited knowledge through the veil or wormhole.

People who have died and literally come back to talk about it, sometimes describe going through a tunnel with light at the end of the tunnel. I have astral traveled and I did go through a tunnel. Could the tunnel be the basis of the exploration of Worm Holes?

In my experience, actually we, live souls and dead souls, share the same space. The notion of wormholes is not necessary. Dimensions make the difference between us. We cannot see another dimension because the vibrations are different. I have experienced the higher, faster vibration of another dimension, a dimension where dead people in spirit are quite alive.

I have been an astral traveler since I was a child sleeping in the same bed as you. Only as an adult have I figured out what was happening when the vibrations would start each time I would relax enough to be going to sleep. I found the vibrations a little uncomfortable but I also had lived with them all my life, so I thought everyone experienced them. There were two vibrations, a rough, lower one would start and then it would change to a quicker, smoother, higher one. Then, off I would go. Only as an adult, do I remember my astral trips in detail and with whom I traveled.

However, I was aware of and saw spirits as a small child. In fact, our parents moved us out of a house because I continually saw a spirit, a man watching me at bedtime in that house before I was two years old.

I am certain there are earth-bound spirits who present as ghosts but that is the mystery of the invisible universe – the ghosts and sounds that continue as though a recording plays over and over. I have also heard those sounds and had experience with ghosts as though an imprint is made on certain places. That is an energy that stays behind and not necessarily a stuck soul. It can be erased or in other words, released by someone who knows how to do it. Aboriginal shamans often can clear the imprint or if it is, in fact, a stuck soul, they can release the soul to move on.

I am certain there is life other than earth life. It is not the material world of other planets. This is different. It is life in different spheres, different vibrations, invisible to us humans, except to the humans who have a kind of portal open to see and experience the invisible life. It is vibrant, more so than here on earth. Life beyond this earthly life is so different and vast that it cannot be accurately explained to our simple linear minds.

I have been there. Taken to another world by very large spirits who lifted me out of my body. The identities of the spirits have been my secret for many years. I may or may not reveal my secret.

We have life all around us, watching over us, ignoring us, teaching us, and invisible to us. It is a misconception to think that if a spirit makes himself/herself known that the spirit is stuck. I have said this to you before as the question came up over and over, implying that my dead husband is stuck and not moving on. Actually he is continuing to be hard at work, healing, protecting, and teaching from his place in our lives. Guardian Angel is a term often used.

I was born with an open portal to the spirit world. In other words, amnesia of the afterlife (or before life) was not complete when I was born. In a lecture I attended in my twenties, Alan Watts asked the question, "Where were you before you were born?" The audience was stunned for a few minutes with the thought. He went on to ask, "If you peel an onion and you get to the centre and it falls away, where is the onion?" I thought about that onion for years. For one thing, the odor is still present, so the onion is not gone.

I have seen countless spirits and talked with them. I have also closed the portal on spirits who wish to be in communication through me because we have the choice to be an open vessel or to choose when and with whom to be open. It is kind of like tuning in to a particular radio frequency. I am tuned into my late husband and will continue to be. He can go about his business of being dead and still very much alive and well, and I can continue to live my life, all the while being tuned into each other. We have come to a place where we honor each other in whatever choices we make now in our lives. He wants me to be free to live my life however I wish.

Then, there is the question of destiny. Information given to me by an invisible being when I was in my twenties, told me many things about my life as yet unfolded at the time. I was told I could not change certain things no matter how I tried because it involved the life and destiny of other people. The information was uncanny and some of it, I would not have wished upon myself or anyone else. What I was told came to pass as years went by and I could not change destiny as it did unfold, even though I did try to change it. I also was told that I would teach people about life after death. Maybe that is what I am doing now.

Just keep in mind we are using a linear thinking mind that finds the non-linear life mind-boggling.

For one thing, I have struggled with trivial questions like: if all things are of God (or the Creator), then sh-t is Holy, too. Is that where the derogatory term "Holy Sh-t" comes from and is it wrong to swear it? I guess it is in what tone it is used. Over the years, I have gone from one silly question to another and the questions have not always been easy ones.

I do not have total understanding, I just have a tiny ... and I mean tiny, experience of the dimension outside earthly life ... just enough to be certain life continues after death. I have been through the wormhole.

Since you passed away, you have appeared to me and you spoke clearly, so I know you continue to live and remember life here.

Now that you are on the other side, maybe you will tell me about wormholes from your point of view.

Your sister

Just another Story

A SECRET REVEALED

I am sleeping. I am awakened into the zone between waking and sleeping. I am very alert.

Albert Einstein appears. I recognize two composers, Ludwig Van Beethoven and Wolfgang Amadeus Mozart, flanking him on either side. The three are in different bodies than we are. They are all larger – much larger and more ethereal. They are so large that I can only see them from their heads to chest, arms and hands. Einstein puts his hand under my feet and gently but firmly lifts me out of my body. I am small on the palm of Einstein's hand.

I am lifted up into my room and through the roof of my house. The sky is clear and stars are shining. We go through the stars and come to a place of light. This is a place of living beings. We pass by my youngest daughter who is lying on her stomach and reading a book while floating in space.

I am pleased because she is just learning to read and here in her astral form, she can already read. She is supposedly in bed sleeping, but here she is in space reading a book!

Einstein takes me to where I meet briefly with my mother. Other members of my family are here, too. My mother and I have a short conversation about very obvious and every day matters of this place, like it is familiar to both of us.

Einstein and I are suddenly the same size as we stand side by side on the outskirts of a city that looks very much like an earthly city. Einstein explains at length and in detail about life there to me.

Einstein always stays slightly to my left. Mozart and Beethoven stay to my right. The composers never speak; they are simply there as companions and all the while I am in awe of their being present for me, though it also seems normal.

Suddenly, I realize that we are floating and I become afraid that my small daughter might fall. This sudden fear ends the astral travel.

I am in my room again with absolutely clear memory of the trip. It is still so vivid that I can feel the pressure of Einstein's hands on my feet and feel the exhilaration of having had a wonderful trip. I realize that I cannot remember the details of my conversations or the details of the place we visited, although I can see still see it clearly from the edge of the city.

These words were impressed on my mind as I lay there in bed. "The kiss of death."

I realized the prophesy of years ago, that I would be shown life after death was definitely coming true.

what followed

The same day that I had the astral travel experience with Albert Einstein, a man who wanted to be recognized as a guru but in my view was really a wannabe, came to the house for a visit. In my excitement I dared to tell him about my experience.

He stared at me and said nothing. The look on his face was like I had just said I went to the bathroom and he wished he had not heard it. I had just laid a dud.

I realized he did not believe me. I decided then, never to talk about my trip with Albert Einstein. It has remained my secret for decades.

Over those decades, I have had questions. Why me? Why would Albert Einstein bother with educating me? Why would two famous composers who are in fact my favorites, come to flank Albert Einstein and me? I looked for clues in my past. Since I was a very small child, I always felt a special bond to Einstein and my ears would perk up at the mention of his name on the radio, although I never knew why and had no early understanding of his work. I always felt a special bond with Beethoven and his music causes me to transcend reality. I only learned later that Mozart was Einstein's favorite composer. Then, I learned that Beethoven admired Mozart in life and wanted to study with him, but Mozart died before he had the chance. So all three had connections in earthly life. I wondered what connection I may have had with these spirits in a former life. I have searched pictures and biographies to find clues.

I became interested in Albert Einstein's questions about time and how mass shapes time. I only had life and people to observe about how time gets shaped by movement. In other words, marking time may not be the same for everyone. Why do some people age fast while others seem to stay young forever? Where is the edge – the border? What if there are no boundaries?

Why me? That question has never been answered. What I do know is that my questions about cosmic energy have no boundaries.

So there it is! Believe or not; it really does not matter.

☆ ☆○ ☆

Just another Story

LUCID DREAMING

A true story: After reading a book about Saint Theresa of Avila, I went to bed and slept through the night. In the morning, on the brink between sleeping and waking, I dreamed that I was dreaming that I was dreaming. With each stage of dreaming I went through deeper levels of consciousness to a state of super consciousness. I was now more acutely awake than in my every day waking consciousness. I heard a choir of a thousand, thousand angels singing, more beautiful and powerful than can be described.

Just another Story

JUST THINKING

This morning, I was on the way to the seaside to think about storytelling. As I was leaving the house, I heard persistent and loud birds. I turned around to see what the commotion was about. High above, in the branches of the tallest tree in my yard, two bald eagles sat side by side. They looked like a pair, female and male. They were both looking directly at me and intently yacking as though telling me something important. I had seen many eagles flying overhead, but never sitting in our tree. I stood there for a long time, just listening with respect to what they were telling me. Maybe somehow, my intuitive mind would get their messages.

Storytelling to me means conveying the effervescent soul of a story that is alive in the fabric of universal energy rather than a stagnant, linear kind of historical event. Hopefully, the eagles have helped me be the best storyteller I can be today.

love and sex

Overwhelmed with how to put into words the many questions and observations of energy at work in daily living, I went to the ocean to sit and think. Seagulls were noisy above the splash of incoming tide on the sand. As I sat there taking it all in, I found it amusing that my list just got longer because tides happen twice a day and are enormous energy.

My mind tends to dwell in the arts, not science, but questions about energy have occupied my mind all my life. Even in playing at the arts, my six-year old granddaughter once said to me as she watched me mixing glazing ingredients, "You are doing science!" She was right. It would take several kinds of energy to complete the project. In calculated amounts, I would use age-old minerals from the earth, water, air and fire.

I came to the seaside to ponder my long list of different kinds of energy and how to tell stories about energy, but the subject of love and sex keeps jumping up, twirling around and shoving everything else aside, wanting to be thought about. What is it about love that is so powerful, so full of energy that it transcends every other emotion and cuts through distance? How is it that love can continue as an emotion even after death and is shared between a living person and a person who has died but lives on as spirit? How is it that we bring into present life, longings of love relationships from past lives? How is it that we recognize a loved one from a past life union? How is it that the emotion of love is so healing? How is it that if a person is not feeling loved by another person, there is an intense craving for love and a feeling of emptiness without it? What transports love – is it light? How is love able to move unseen across time and space?

The word love is used in many ways. "I will love you if you do what I want." Or, "I do love you because you behave the way I want you to behave." Is it love when a person revengefully destroys a so-called loved one? Romantic love can often be an allotted time span in which attachment either grows or disappears according to changing looks, smells, or simply someone else crossing a path and becoming a replacement romantic entanglement; is this really love or is it a fickle and fleeting masquerade of love?

True love is unconditional and everlasting. Pure love has no boundaries. Love is complete within itself.

crazy women

As a romantic teenager, I carried a book of Greek myths under my arm. With no sexual knowledge of my own, the stories gave something to dream about. I ignored the wars, jealousies, and revenge in the myths; instead, I fantasized about mystical, invisible lovers. I concentrated on Leda and the Swan, and Psyche and Cupid in their loving, sexual encounters, and wondered where the stories came from. I questioned what life experience would create these imagined stories.

Oh, the stories I have heard!

"I have a spirit lover." I heard that phrase several times from different women. The stories are similar in that the women found satisfaction in having an invisible lover. Each woman thought her experience was unique.

One woman, a dancer, was uncertain in the beginning about her safety in having an invisible lover making love to her at night when she slept in her dance studio. When she talked about it, she became comfortable and vowed to continue instead of running home where her lover seemed not to follow.

Another woman was feeling unloved in her marriage. Her invisible lover gave her a new sense of enjoyment in life. A dapper man would appear dressed in formal clothing and a top hat. His attire was opposite of the clothing people wore on the farms around her. She was not prepared to share the information about her lover with her husband; she knew he would be jealous despite being emotionally distant from her.

Another woman was a widow. As soon as her husband passed away, she could feel him play with her body. She knew him by a feeling and a unique knowing that two longtime lovers have with each other. She was amused because now he could play with her body day and night, so long as she allowed it. She allowed it even while she was working. Nightly, he would make serious love with her. She could feel him as clearly as if he was in his body with all his body parts. Her only question was how come he had all his body parts and his desire to continue making love with her.

Sexual union of two bodies for some people is love and why the act of becoming one is called lovemaking. In listening to these women, the question I had was, in what fiber of the universe is love and is the fiber really all love. Is that what our universe is made of? After all, love is in all animals as well as humans. It is a universal feeling that is retained eternally no matter what else happens in life.

Saint Teresa of Avila was known to have nightly rapturous experiences. She talked about and later wrote about the rapture of her physical body brought by angels that she saw in visions; she experienced one as a lover piercing her body from her heart to her bowels. These experiences brought jealousy and criticism on her head. There were those who thought she was possessed by the Devil. Priests and teachers gave advice on how she should pray to clean herself of these rapturous experiences.

Sex between spirits and humans has been taboo in many cultures. The rapturous sexual encounters in our world of everyday living have long been hidden. Learned people who have not had the personal experience of an invisible lover, do not believe it possible and worse, they say it is madness when spoken about.

Lovemaking between humans and spirits has been a hidden, scary and forbidden subject. People rarely admit to having a secret lover that is invisible, or to being made love to and experiencing extreme rapture with an unseen lover. Being thought of as delusional, mentally ill, and then possibly rejected from friends and society keep people from telling about their secret lovers.

Why do we believe that life as known on earth is left behind when a person dies? What if life continues with memories intact? What if human emotions, lust, and love of the human body also are carried over? What if attachment between the soul of a departed and a companion left behind actually continues? What if that continuous love is of a sexual nature?

Love carries energy and so does light carry energy. Life must have the ingredient of light energy and healthy life must have love. Life is not just grey matter of the physical form. When love disappears, the world becomes barren. When light disappears from the physical body, body part, or plant, the result is a return to earth.

Every living thing needs water. When a plant refuses to drink water, death will follow. Now here is a thought: in death, light disappears from the physical body but carries on, allowing a soul to manifest and be seen as light. However, love is a feeling that is constant and strong even without manifested light.

The earth needs water in order to survive, as we know it. Water, according to some researchers, does carry memory and can be imprinted.

Water can be found by dowsing with a willow twig. The willow loves water and will point the way, reaching, tugging and dipping to tell the dowser how deep under ground, how much, what color, and in what direction the water flows. The energy between the two acts like a magnet.

prayer

Thoughts are carried by energy without words. All words, sounds of mantras, and prayers are living in the fabric of the universe. Sound is carried across space. Why is prayer used around the world no matter what religion or belief in a God or Creator? Why is prayer so powerful?

As a ten year old, that question became important. It was winter on the prairies. My family had supper at seven o'clock every evening because my father had to be at work by eight. This did not fit my schedule. I would sneak out of the house with my skates and head to the outdoor rink a few blocks from my home. My mother asked me nicely a few times to stay for supper and then go skating. I was an outdoor kid no matter if the weather was nice or blizzardy and I wanted to be at the skating rink during the whole evening. Then she got serious and threatened me with a good licken if I snuck out again. After the first threat, I did it again. After nine o'clock, I prayed all the way home and promised not to do it again if only my mother would not hit me. I got home and to my surprise, my prayer seemed to work. My mother was nice to me but threatened if I did it again that she would have to carry out the licken.

Well, the next night, I grabbed my skates and snuck out again before supper. On the way home, I prayed again and promised not to do it again if only my mother would not hit me. When I got home, my mother simply threatened again but did nothing. I was convinced my prayers were working. Whew!

Well, I did it again on the third evening. I prayed again on my way home and made the same promise. Only this time, I had a strong feeling that someone was listening and that someone was not pleased about me telling lies in my prayers.

When I got home, my mother was upset that finally she would have to carry out her threat and hit me. She took me to the basement where my brothers and sister could not see, and she gave me a few good wallops on my rear end with a belt. It hurt.

I would never give anyone the satisfaction of seeing me cry. My mother was the kindest, gentlest person. She cried because she hurt me. I did not. But I did quit sneaking out before supper because I felt sorry for my mother.

The question I thought a lot about, was: Who was listening? And who was the presence that I felt was the judge of whether I lied or not?

I remember only two lickens in my childhood, one from my mother and then one from my father. Both lickens were because of prayer.

I was twelve when my father suddenly decided we would become a family that prays together. One Sunday evening, he lined up the family in the living room to pray. I refused to participate. I felt that my prayers were too private to be on display. Stubbornly, I took off to a side room. Actually, it was the room I could hide in when I needed to cry and no one would find me. The family prayed but when they were finished, my father came looking for me. He took me out to the living room to make an example of what he thought about atheism, or at least about my stubbornness. In front of my family still in a lineup to watch, my father who had all my life been my best friend, spanked me hard on my rear end. I stubbornly would not cry in front of anyone. This was the first and only time my father ever laid a hand on me. It upset him so much that he gave up and never again made the family line up to pray.

My father and I continued our close friendship. He was a man of stories and more than anyone else I could listen endlessly to his stories. When learning arts and crafts, I always made gifts for my father.

On his deathbed, my father asked me if he was a good father.

How could I tell my father in words how I appreciated what he had done for me? Being his oldest child, I got the best of him.

As a three year old, I learned how protective my father was of me. One afternoon, I was missing. He rode the neighborhood on his bicycle until he found me lying under a bush with my pants down. An older girl was about to invade my body.

With the sun over his head and shining through his hair, giving him a golden glow, I looked into my father's face. He gathered me up and put me on his bicycle. On the ride home, he explained the birds and bees to me so that he could be sure I understood that I should never let anyone do that to me again.

I do not remember how I got into that situation, but I remember clearly the moment my father appeared and the ride home. I remember the feeling of absolute protection. The world felt safe.

He enjoyed teaching me how to read, write and do mathematics long before I went to school. He encouraged me to be an artist and taught me ballroom dancing. He sat through my piano recitals as a proud father whether I played well or not. While my mother taught cooking and sewing, and took me to the Conservatory piano exams, my father taught me joys of being wild and free outdoors. He taught me how to ride horses, to skate, to ride a bicycle, to swim. He bragged endlessly to anyone who would listen about how I caught bigger fish than he caught when we ice fished together.

When he was dying, I arrived and he told me he was afraid I would not be able to come. It meant a lot to him that I was there. While I sat beside him for days, we listened to music and watched horseracing on the television. Music and horses were shared enjoyments for both of us all our lives. While we listened to his famous second-cousin play his music, I asked my father why, when he had been given the offer to go off with his cousin and play music, he did not go.

My father answered, "I had a wife and children. I had a job. I had everything I wanted in life. Money and fame would not have given me more."

To me, he really was a good father. He died soon after I said he was. After all that my father had done for me, I forgot to apologize to my father for refusing to pray with him.

☆

A little bit off topic; this brings up the only other spanking I remember ever happening in my house. I caused it. I hated liver and I hated cooked carrots. I had flushed my liver down the toilet and plugged it; I got away with that. I hid my carrots behind the bathtub and it was not the first time. My mother found them and asked who put them there. I knew she knew it was me, but my sister quickly said she did it. I was really surprised she would cover for me and thought she was stupid for doing so. My mother immediately gave her a spanking, not because of my carrots, but because my sister lied and said she did it. I was made to clean up my mess as my punishment.

Over years, I have asked my sister several times why she wanted to cover for me. She has no explanation other than she was a well-behaved kid never in trouble. I always got into trouble and she thought, "Oh, here we go again." She felt sorry for me because of carrots. So this story stays in the fabric of the universe. I am still giving it energy!

is there higher power

Is there a higher power, an intelligence that can respond to prayer?

I woke up in hospital with a nurse by my side, a bag of blood attached to a pole and a tube attached to my arm. She fiddled with settings on the tubes to start the flow to me and disappeared.

I could feel the transfusion come to me too cold and too fast. My body could not handle it. I immediately went into shock and suddenly I was ill to an extreme. My body let fluids fly from all ends. I was so ill that I was convinced there was a bottom of illness and I was in it.

I prayed silently for help.

I felt a presence. I felt a response. Immediately, I was totally well and peaceful in a kind of peace and light that seemed unworldly. It only lasted a few seconds.

A thought was impressed upon me, "You need to go through this."

Then, as quickly as I was well, I was again in shock and ill as before. I was continuing to throw up. The cold blood was unbearable.

The nurse came in. She was furious with me for making a mess and for having to clean up.

I tried to explain that the blood infusion was too fast and too cold, but that tough, mean lady was not about to listen to anything I had to say. Not only that, but when I came to and was functioning, I found out that in the room next door was a patient with a raging illness that was contagious. The door between the two rooms had been open all that time and this same nurse was going between the two rooms without washing her hands.

I did recover completely in a few days and went home feeling grateful to have survived despite the nurse and that I did not get the other patient's illness.

The experience left me with a feeling about nursing. Patients are vulnerable and should be respected even when no one is watching.

Since that experience, I have carried with me a knowing that there has to be a higher, invisible intelligence. I was heard. I was responded to. I was given a brief healing so that I would know I was heard. I was also given a partial reason for my suffering, but that reason just leads to more questions.

dreams

Since I was a child, I wondered how dreams took a person into action packed situations where known people became different in a dream. How are dreams able to tell of future events if the future had not yet happened? What is time when dreams seem to have no time? Anything and everything can happen in odd timing, upside down timing, ageless time, yesterday and future timing. In a dream, a person can be a child reliving a present life or another life. What about recurring themes in dreams? And how is it that an answer to a question can be found in a dream?

Some people are at work when at rest, either daydreaming or dream dreaming. Einstein was a good example of a person at work when he was lying in his boat and relaxing. I have that habit. When I look like I am relaxing, I am often hard at work and may suddenly jump up to put into action what I was working on.

What about the dreams where two people dream the same dream? That has happened to my daughter and me. In the middle of the night, I woke up out of a dream and found my daughter wandering the hallway. She told me about her dream that woke her up and I had just had the exact same dream. Our deceased loved one, my mother/her grandmother appeared in our dreams and gave each of us at the exact same time, specific instructions about what she wanted done with her ashes; this followed differing opinions expressed by other family members. In the end, regardless of other opinions, my father made plans to do exactly what his wife had asked for in our dreams.

What about messages given by a living or deceased person? We had not told our father of our dreams. Somehow, he completed a triangle and carried her wishes through.

What about lucid dreaming that is different and more vivid than most dreams?

A woman had questions in therapy about a recurring dream that she was a male pirate on a ship. As she talked, I could see the pirate as though I was looking through her present person to the person in her dreams. It seemed that she was continuing to work out certain problems that carried over from her past life through the drama of dreams. In this life, she was born into a female body but carried the mind-set of a male. She told many stories of her activities as an active lesbian always searching out a sexual encounter as though the piracy was still active in her.

I was woken out of deep sleep in the middle of the night because someone was touching my body. Awake, I was fully aware that this same person in astral form had invaded my bedroom by astral travel. She was attempting to have a sexual encounter with me. I immediately closed her out and got rid of her. I did not share her sexual preferences. She had not been invited by me and never would be. I felt violated.

I did not know if she was fully aware of what she had done while astral traveling. What I knew for sure now was that she had a desire to be sexual with me. She apparently still carried the mind-set of a pirate and I was fair game for rape. I was so incensed that I refused to have even a brief follow-up meeting with her. In working in medicine, I could tolerate a lot, but my mind, body and spirit were not available for stealing.

What about astral travel? It is reported that dreams of falling are actually the return of the soul to the body in a rather clumsy fashion. Anyone who has astral traveled tells stories that to them are real and true. These travelers accept no disputing arguments because they know what they know.

What are dreams made of? Are they not solid form but simply pictures in the brain, or are they activity happening in another dimension and remembered as light forms in the memory part of the brain – or can they simply be remembered feelings with no picture memory and maybe translated into pictures? There are no definitive answers, only theories.

waves of energy

On what radio wave does thought travel? How can emotion be transmitted across the fabric of space? What is the transport? Light? Love? How is it able to move unseen across time and space and yet be real? Now we have radio, television and telephones that are wireless not just on earth, but also from spaceships far out into space as far as the planet Mars, while traveling at great speed.

What about sound? Why is it that music sounds correct and pleasing to the ear when it is mathematically correct? If the musical notes are not mathematically in order, it is called discordant; meaning the sound is inharmonious and unpleasant.

The vibrations of sound in tuning musical instruments are mathematically tuned within the instrument and then to be in tune with other instruments, the mathematical vibrations must be the same. When learning to play a musical instrument, we learn intuitive mathematics of sound.

There is a mathematical consistency in the rhythm of incoming waves of the ocean, forming music on the sand in front of me as I sit here, listening to nature.

Sound can be heard and felt, but is invisible. Sound is so powerful that it can break glass and cause metal to fatigue. A speeding airplane that breaks the sound barrier can cause havoc. I have been below a broken sound barrier; the invisible waves from the boom caused my house to shake. I have broken a video editing machine with horn and drum vibrations at a level the machine could not handle.

Thought transfer is done all the time. Often, picking up thoughts of another person comes in a feeling or a quick picture that stops us in our tracks momentarily to wonder where that came from. Intuition receives transferred thoughts when the mind is calm or in tiny cracks between mumbo-jumbo busyness. Most of us have had intuitive thoughts that are information about a loved one.

Animals respond to our thoughts and emotions while being present and from great distances; this is especially evident when an animal is attached to a person as a pet.

Intuition crosses time and space. There is no barrier except in the individual who is closed, and that is where we might find skeptics to the paranormal.

Objects hold imprints of whatever touches them. Color affects whatever it shines upon. Under the canopy of green trees, we feel the green, we breath the green right into our body, and we have green tones on our skin. In other words, we are energy that is without solid lines or barriers.

We are the energy of our surroundings, invisible and visible.

Is this what is meant when we are told that God, the Creator is in each of us ... that we are at one with the Creator? Just thinking ...

Just another Story

CONFESSIONS BY THE SEA

losing armor

Working in medicine, I have witnessed the spectrum of beginning life and ending life, and heard many variations of love, sex and crime in stories. Stories by the sea are different in that they do not expect the listener to fix anything.

It seems the sea is a magnet for people to spill their stories into the vastness of the cleansing waters. Strangers will tell each other stories by the ocean, even though they may never meet again. The pendulum of stories swings widely from small secret confessions of sorrow and happiness to life-changing stories of great heart-wrenching significance.

At the waterfront, there are meetings with old friends. Always, there are the lonely people looking for companionship for a few minutes but might be hoping to stretch the time for a long relationship.

As I sit on a log with my feet in the sand and feeling the fresh salty air on my face, I listen to whoever stops by.

On a warm summer evening that started out just watching colors of the sunset, I sat for hours that lasted into the blackened night when only the moon shone on silvery waves. It was well past midnight before this heart wrenching, life-changing confession was finished. In that setting, her tears blended with the water of the sea and the salty air. It seemed the story would go on forever somewhere in cosmic energy. Because of the many layers in the story, it is included in this story circle.

On a hot, sunny late Spring day, she drove to the forest where she and her small dog could walk under the canopy of cool green.

When she started her car to leave, it made a noise and a dashboard warning came on. In the past, the illusive warning would disappear by the time she got to the car service centre. So, this time, she ignored the dashboard and drove down the hill, across a major intersection, and onto a busy artery into her neighborhood.

Halfway up a steep hill that was several blocks long, car power faded and quit. The car immediately started to roll backward down the hill. The brakes did not work. She turned the key to off and applied emergency brakes and blinkers. She turned the key to start and disengaged the emergency brakes. There was nothing. The car started to roll backward. She went through the routine three times, as though she did not believe what was happening. Only the emergency brakes were keeping her stuck to the hill.

If they gave out, she would slide backward out of control into traffic. She was relying on blinkers to warn other cars.

Being overly independent, nothing ever scared her, but today she was facing fear. With all the weight of a heavy car completely dependent on a cable for emergency brakes, she was afraid of rolling backward out of control and causing many people to get hurt or even killed. Watching through the rearview mirror, she was afraid of the cars seemingly oblivious that she was unable to move out of their way. Lines of vehicles were whizzing by at terrific speeds. Some swerved around only a few feet from her at the last minute.

She kept a cell phone only for emergencies, but it was usually forgotten at home or tossed in the back seat and sometimes in the trunk, out of reach. She was able to reach the cell phone. Now she felt scared and lucky.

Minutes later, through her rearview mirror, she could see the tow truck coming in a determined way up the hill toward her. It sped past and quickly positioned in front of her. The driver was precise, not having to adjust an inch.

A middle-aged man with fair hair jumped out of his vehicle and was swiftly at her side, looking at her through the open window. His smile, his friendly eyes, his presence surrounded her with warmth and protection. Fear fled. In a split second, as she looked into his eyes, she lost armor. It was as though she split wide open. Her inner core was bare. She felt his aura wrapped around her, holding her safe.

"I'm so glad to see you!" Those words were probably the truest of her life. "What do I do now?"

In a soft confident voice, he gave instructions, guiding her to safely exit the car and run to the curbside to take her dog out while he stayed on the road to safeguard her exit.

She watched, marveling at how he worked efficiently and quickly to secure her car. But internally, at the same time as she stood there on the street watching him, her whole life was flashing very fast in front of her. Her armor had just been shattered; she was now forced to see and accept reality of past relationships that were different than rosy pictures she had preferred.

She was acutely aware that her inner core was naked and this man who was helping her had just gotten past her defenses.

Then, as a gentleman, he guided her into his truck. She held her dog on her lap. They were out of danger.

As they drove away, conversation was comfortable and genuine.

This man not only saved her from whatever but now he knew just how to help her to relax into the comedy of her situation.

They were headed to the car service centre where there would be many people. She was unfit to be in public because she was in old and clingy rayon pajama bottoms, no bra under a skimpy blouse, no mascara, and she had no idea what her hair looked like. New running shoes were the only publicly decent things she was wearing. After all, she had only been going to walk in the forest where no one would see her, except black bears, coyotes, deer, cougars and eagles. She had intended to shower after she got home.

She remarked to him about her embarrassed comedy and that now she understood why women might expect the unexpected and dress up for walking their dogs.

He was amused and agreed.

When they arrived at the destination, she was hoping to stop far away from anyone able to see her get out of the truck, but he made a deliberate detour around the parking lot to the main door. He hopped out of the truck and made his way quickly around to help her out safely.

It was a long way down. She slid out but had to turn around to grab her dog from the seat. She realized her hind-end was facing the giant glass windows and her lightweight pants allowed clear view of her hind-end contour. The problem was that she was aware of a certain man who worked at his computer by the window and she hoped he was not looking. She was embarrassed but she would think about that later.

She thanked her guardian angel and they said their goodbyes. She watched as he parked her car with precision in a tight spot. As she watched, she wondered why he had stirred her so deeply.

She would take the experience home with her and over the next few days, she would mull the meeting over and over, trying to make sense of what happened to her. Had it been because she was so vulnerable in a dangerous situation on the side of a hill? He had plucked her from extreme danger. He had guided her, making her feel safe every minute of his presence. The conversation between them had been easy, as though they had known each other forever and left her wanting more, but she would not hold her breath waiting for that.

The bonding energy had been tangible. Then he was gone.

She mused that for a few minutes they had looked at each other through rose-colored glasses. It had been like looking at each other through a portal of timelessness.

In days and months later, she would fleetingly see him pass by while he was doing the work of guardian angel to other people in distress. She would wonder about him.

In order to make some sense of what happened, she would decide it was her capacity for unconditional love of humanity that allowed her to open up to this man and be vulnerable emotionally. Two souls had come together that day and then parted. What contact with this man had done for her in a split second was to reawaken the whole woman. Now, without her armor, she would never be the same again.

She will never speak to him of what happened for her that day. She will never know if he gave her a second thought but accepts 'probably not'. She will never know ... but she does know she is very alive in every sense.

He will never know how he stirred the heart of a woman. He will never know how he was briefly in the presence of timeless love. He will never know how he became just another story. When he sits in his truck, all alone, wondering about life and love, he will never know ...

confession

She and her dog arrived at her car's place of service at noon of a busy day. As she got out of the tow truck, she had to reach in for her dog. She realized her scantily clad rear-end faced the floor to ceiling windows but she could not change that right now. Without even looking behind her, she could feel the presence of a service advisor she had dealt with before. He was a gentle man and always gave excellent care to his clients. She knew he was sitting near the window at his computer. She did not want to look at him and hoped to get by him unnoticed.

The place was busy with a lot of clients milling around centre floor and because she was with her dog and had been dropped off at the glass doors by a tow truck, people did notice. Several service advisors were at their desks. She could feel the strong physical presence like a magnet of the service advisor she was avoiding. She walked to the opposite side of the room but glanced back just momentarily so as not to be caught looking at him. She turned her back on him again, not wanting to face him in her disarray. But it flashed through her mind that she had ignored him in past maintenance appointments also, and each time she had looked at him longingly from across the crowded room.

Her blouse slid off her shoulder and down her arm. She pulled it up, but it fell down again. After several tries to keep her blouse from slipping off her shoulder, she gave up and let it be. She stood there with her partly bare back to him, remembering the circumstances around the first time she ever saw him. She had spent the previous years nursing her husband in his illness and he died just three weeks before she came for car service. It had been a difficult time having to be brave and strong. She was tired from the years lacking sleep while not being able to fix anything. Just a week ago, her daughter had married. The wedding was too large to change the date. There had been a funeral and a wedding in just two weeks. In both events she had to play a major role in public – a widow and mother of the bride.

Meanwhile, her car had a recall and it had been necessary to have the car repaired before starting the new job the following week that she had very reluctantly accepted. Emotionally, it would be tough. She felt like she had gone to the moon to live. Nothing seemed familiar. In that fog, she had hardly been in a mood to be interested in another man. But she wondered now, why even under those absurdly difficult circumstances, the man she was avoiding had impressed her enough to remember clearly seeing him for the first time a dozen years ago. She remembered his face, his hair, the feel of him. Considering that no other person stood out from that time, she pondered the question for a few minutes in the midst of people doing business.

Bringing her mind back to the present day, she sought the help of a new service advisor that she found less unsettling and where her unkempt bedroom appearance would not matter so much.

Weeks later, the new advisor was out to lunch when she returned for additional maintenance. The man she had been avoiding asked if he could help. She started to object. He smiled. She melted. That was the start. Softly and carefully, he took the time to explain overall car care. She understood for the first time and wished she had never turned her back on him – ever.

On return, she asked him if he minded her calling him exclusively. He stood up. His face lit up with a burst of boyishness that caught her off-guard. His kind soul was exposed. She felt something like a lightening bolt striking her. She kept a well-practiced straight face but she was shaken to her exposed core. Suddenly she knew why she had avoided him in the past; he was the sexiest, most desirable man on earth. She wanted to melt right into his maleness. His chest drew her to him. His face, in those moments, became vividly imprinted deep within her. A transformation was happening. She could not yet understand the totality of what was happening.

What had been an innocent request just a minute ago for the best car service had just changed everything and she would be unable to undo it.

Because she had guests arriving from out of town, she decided to wait the couple of hours for her car; waiting would allow her to get home quicker than going and coming back by a courtesy car.

From the archway of the waiting room, she watched him working hour after hour. This was the first time she was willing to just relax and watch him; this was her undoing.

The way he moved as he worked was drawing on her; his masculinity was magnetizing. When he walked across the room and stood in front of a vending machine, she had a profound awakening of memories. She suddenly found herself craving to hug his body that felt familiar – known. She recognized him as home. He and she had been together before in unconditional love without boundaries, through eons. She had been missing him from what seemed like the day she was born. She loved him, pure and simply, like no other she had ever known in this lifetime. Now, she knew that her life would never be the same again.

When he came to explain the work done, he leaned over the table to read from his papers. Only inches from him, she watched his face carefully. Everything about him pleased her. She wanted to touch his bottom lip. It was hard not to reach out and touch him, and take him into her arms. In the closeness, she allowed him into her softest, inner core. At the end of his explanation, he smiled, almost shyly. Maybe he felt her watching him.

The craving to see him again stayed strong over weeks. He had taken up residence in her heart.

She was now openly recognizing him. He was the love of her spirit, now reawakened in a body that flamed in craving. His vibrations would come in waves. She understood now that avoiding this man for years had been a conscious strategy. She had ignored him deliberately and walked past him on several occasions without acknowledging him because she had been attracted to him.

When her car showed signs of trouble the following week, he obliged quickly by going out to her car to listen to noises she was hearing. While he was sitting in the car, she realized the desire to caress his hair as she watched him work. She managed to check herself and not do the unthinkable. In all her life, she had never felt so out of control over a man. This was entirely different.

She had dared to really look at him. He was a large man, somewhere in his middle age. She knew he was a gentle soul and at the same time, manly energetic. She had allowed his smile to warm her. He was no longer the younger man, she now felt younger than him and so very vulnerably female. She was overcome with emotions of wanting to put her arms around his body, to hold him close and sooth whatever needed to be soothed. Her whole body wanted to wrap around him and keep him safe.

It had become increasingly difficult to leave him and go home without saying a word.

Emotionally, being a faithful widow was over. She was suddenly longing for love and companionship.

She was alone to sort out her feelings. Her shell was still missing. She was like mush with no outer protection. Facing wild animals in the forest seemed a breeze compared to this.

She had always had a few nevers in her life. Never this. Never that. Never ... never ... never take a lover younger than herself. She never wanted to grow old and lose her lover to a younger woman, or simply, never to face rejection again. So, never had been safe. Having privately faced her own past in that moment when her shell cracked open, she was now letting go of never-never land, but with nothing tangible to land on.

Feeling the pangs of love with the empty, hurt feelings that go with such a dilemma, she craved to feel his body. She convinced herself that just one physical hug by his warm body would make her feel better and satisfied for the rest of her life. She wanted just a minute close to his face to look into his eyes. She wanted – needed to feel his energy. Just to sit next to him away from his work and be friends having a conversation would suffice. She craved to be able to talk with him and know his life. Bargaining with the universe, she begged for anything other than this emptiness.

Her overactive physical passion and craving raged on day and night. What happened? This was an accident! She had not meant it to happen! Her admiration of him had, in a flash of awakened memory, turned into full-blown love. With the recognition, came extreme longing and craving for physical love ... closeness, touching, fiery bodies becoming one.

In rational moments, the only thing she knew was that jeopardizing their new friendship with a declaration was not what she wanted to do. She wanted to keep him in her life and not scare him off. Most of all, she did not want to hurt him or anyone close to him because she had no knowledge about what his private life was like. She could not imagine such a gentle, sexy man being single.

She was now hurting with yearning for an unattainable man and the thought of not ever really knowing him in this life hurt deeply. On the other hand, the thought of being hurt or hurting him with an unwanted encounter was even more unbearable.

"Why? Why?" she asked the ceiling of her room. "How did this happen?"

Her heart hurt at the thought of not knowing him or of knowing him and losing him, or worse – being rejected. She would have to be safe, even now. She must put the broken shell together again – somehow.

She wondered how many people walk around with a permanent shell and never really look at it. Now she was forced to look because it was broken. What she saw was that she had been blindsided. On a day when she was wide open with fear like none before, a guardian angel arrived, protecting and saving her. She had been raw and innocent as though newborn – the core of her being exposed. Then the guardian angel disappeared; he was not meant to stay. The exposed core was for this man to be seen and to come into her heart again.

Waking up the morning of the appointment with a technician because the car was showing increasing signs of trouble, she was overwhelmed with deep sadness that this would be the last day of seeing her service advisor. She could not understand why she would lose him today.

At the appointment time, he greeted her warmly by her first name and asked how she was. Her heart leapt that he had gotten a tiny bit personal and even remembered her name. She went home thinking the car would be ready the next day and she would see him then.

A couple of hours after dropping off the car, he phoned to say the car repairs would cost more than she was prepared to pay for an old car. She gasped, knowing it was long overdue. He apologized for being the bearer of bad news. She wanted to ease his concerns but she really wanted to tell him she was more upset over losing him than of losing her car. Of course, she said nothing about her feelings and that was that.

He offered a pickup courtesy car for her to return to his office.

Fate played a role now. She waited and watched the clock. The hours ticked by. He would be leaving work if the car did not hurry. The courtesy car never arrived. Just before final closing time, a maintenance person arrived to take her to an office empty of people so that she could drive her limping car home.

The premonition of that morning had been true; he was gone and she had no clue to where he disappeared. The emptiness was too much. Her whole body ached with grief. She told herself it was all for the best. She sent prayers out for his safekeeping. She now loved him so completely, so unconditionally, that she only wanted him to be safe and loved even if she never could see him again. She accepted that he had again become a never in her life.

"The End?" I had asked.
The end? The teller of the story told me that the story should have ended that day but it did not.

When she went to pick up her old car that evening, she looked across the showroom and in another strange flash of intuition, it was as though her name was already on a particular car. Looking at other cars or test-driving was not necessary. By the end of the next day, she drove the new car home with her name on it.

That night she could not sleep. Excitement and disbelief of owning a new car kept her up all night. She used the night to write a story about her love for the younger man.

Writing the story allowed her to unleash pent up feelings of love. She wrote freely about awakening memories of her beloved. In the privacy of her writing, there was no doubt about who he and she were together.

The problem came the next day when she went to the service department. She thought he might be feeling awful after delivering the bad news. All she wanted to do was to let him know that all was well and he should not worry about her.

He was surprised at her sudden appearance. He seemed kind of sad. While shuffling papers, he asked, "What is happening?

"I have a car," she simply said.

He straightened in surprise and seemed to have lost a concern. He looked toward the windows and asked, "Where is it?"

She pointed, "Over there."

"Let's see it."

With enthusiasm, he rounded the counter and together they headed out the doors at a fast pace.

Outside, he asked, "Did they treat you well?" Meaning did the men in sales treat her well.

She was stunned that he cared. She was not used to a man ever asking her that kind of caring question. Glancing sideways at him, she unraveled internally; her knees nearly buckled at the sight of this manly man caring about her. Somehow, she continued to travel fast at his side while explaining how well she had been treated. But, she was also fast losing control of her emotions. She could not overcome her swelling feelings for this man who cared enough to ask. When he asked her another simple question, she could no longer answer.

By the time they got to the car and he expressed his appreciation, and she briefly explained the terms of the surprising car deal, she was now overwhelmed with feelings of pure love for this man. Her love was now acting like a balloon being blown up to a bursting point. In that moment she loved so completely that she lost herself into unconditional love for everyone in the whole world. She understood unconditional love completely.

As they admired her car, her own ego became present again. She was suddenly sad, realizing this car would need little in the way of service. Rather than feeling happy, she was now missing him.

Out of control, she turned to face him. Looking a long way up to his face, she blurted, "I'll miss you."

What she wanted to say is that she had been missing him all her life and that she missed him from her very core, and missing him in future would be unbearable ... and besides ... there was so much to say that was still unsaid. She craved for him to be at her side, to be able to talk together about life, not just about cars.

Surprised, he assured her he would be there for every required six-month service. He was a perfect gentleman, gently reassuring her.

Even more out of control, she reached to touch him, wanting to grab him and hug him and never let him go. Her hand landed somewhere around his waist at his back and she could not believe that she had actually managed to touch his body after all the weeks of craving she had done. He felt so good!

He looked down at her in greater surprise but stood still, not moving a muscle. She caught amusement in his eyes. She managed not to hug him but instead, rubbed him a little where her hand had landed, pretending it to be just an innocent, friendly touch.

Embarrassed now and wanting to correct the situation, she said, "Knowing you is good." She took her hand away but the thrill of touching him was strong; her whole arm had come alive with him.

Looking straight ahead, over her, he again assured her that he would be there for the six-month services. He turned quickly and walked away fast as he again assured her over his shoulder that he would be there "every six months".

Feeling rejected, and knowing she did wrong by almost tackling him in the parking lot of his work, she got in her car and drove away, ending a brief but emotionally explosive time of getting close to him. As she drove away, she remembered that surveillance cameras were probably monitoring the situation. Embarrassment peaked. She had managed to do what all her life she had wanted to avoid. In an emotional outburst, she had just been rejected and she had ruined a good almost-friendship to the point that he ran away. She would not be able to face him again, even for car service.

"The End?" I asked again.

The storyteller breathed deep. There was a long pause as she looked into the sky and beyond into some unlimited place. The writer of this book thought the story had ended. Then the woman's story took another turn ...

All her life she had protected her dignity; now she was out of character. The children's poem, Humpty Dumpty kept running though her mind. Here she was with a broken shell and everything soft inside pouring out. Where were all the king's horses and all the king's men to try to put her together again? She needed help to get her shell together again.

A lifelong positive attitude took over. A solution came to her.

"I can dream. He will be in my dreams," she said to no one but herself. "I'll dream about him. Time does not exist in dreams. And I can't hurt anyone by dreaming."

She did have a dream that very night. He came to her. They talked. But on waking, she could not remember what they spoke about. In another dream, he was a teacher in a schoolroom where she was a visitor but he asked for her help with the children, in fact leaving her in charge while he was busy. She imagined that somewhere in his life he is a caretaker and some kind of teacher.

After several dreams of him coming to her, she dreamed she went to him as he slept. She put her hand on his head, caressing his forehead, then his cheek. Over the months, she had craved to touch his hair and could not; now she could run her fingers through his hair and caress his head. She could touch his lips, his beautiful bottom lip that she had craved to touch. She could lay her head on his chest – the chest she craved to melt into. Then she would wake up. Her body would be on fire with desire.

All her life she had a lively sexual libido that was a driving force. Now it kept her awake with a fierce fire of desire. She desired to know every inch of his physical body. She wanted to touch every inch of his body. She wanted to be with him in reality and make love with him, sleep with him and wake up making love intermittently just as they desired by the moment. She wanted to know him inside and out with unconditional love.

In her dreams, she went to her man night after night and caressed him while he slept.

He started coming to her again. In one lucid dream, he held her close and looked at her with unfathomable tenderness. He swooped her up and carried her to his bedroom with the intention of making love. In the bedroom, children were playing on the bed, and more children were in every room of the house. Lovemaking had to wait. So they went for a walk with a little boy. The little boy's white shoes that he wore were important. The man was carrying a second pair of the boy's shoes that were brown. He handed the brown shoes to her to carry for him.

Looking tired, he wanted her to share his responsibility for the boy and for the other children. She accepted and carried the brown shoes for him.

In most dreams, memories awakened. They were young lovers, ageless in spirit, together forever.

On waking, she thought about the meaning of her dreams. Age difference is an earthly phenomenon but has no place in the realm of spirit. In the timeless universe outside of the material world of earth, souls are free of illnesses and of aging. Birthdates have no meaning there.

Night after night, day after day, they met as lovers in her dreams. An unworldly light surrounded them when he lifted her up to be close to him. Fire raged between them. Their bodies were real. Feelings were intense and at the same time, peaceful. She was in complete ecstasy just being with him.

He was in most of her dreams. They talked a lot. In earthly time by day, she still could never remember what they talked about. She could only remember being with him.

By day, they were having no contact in the physical world now. Sometime, she wondered if it was all her imagination that made the dreams happen and that he had no knowledge of the dreams. Would she ever know? She may never know. She did know that she would never again put him or herself in a situation like she had done in the parking lot. She continued to be embarrassed about being emotionally out of control, but if he came close, she imagined being overwhelmed again and finding it hard not to touch him again. She imagined that he thought of her as a woman on the make, or just out of her mind, and that he had no idea of who she really was in her passionate, ageless inner life.

She continued to wonder if she could ever face him again. She even wondered who else at his work knew about her outrageous behavior. As weeks and months went by, it seemed less likely that she could go back ... ever.

She realized that though she had cared for others in the past, she never loved a man like now. Her love for this man was so entirely different. It was soft and complete. It was unconditional. Just to have him in her life as a close friend and share life stories would suffice. Just to see him smile or to share his problems would be good. But, there seemed to be no way to approach him again even for a friendship; it would have to be up to him and there was no sign that he would be interested.

It seemed that finding car service elsewhere was an option and hopefully, in time, if she did not see or hear him, the heartache of intense craving for having some sort of close friendship would diminish.

She did decide that unless he showed recognition of her, he was better off without her interference ... even in dreams. She wanted to be sure he was free of her and able to live his life, as he should. She was determined to stop the dreams. He had again become a never.

Watched with anxiety, the odometer was creeping up to the service time. Walking away would be personally extremely difficult and hurt a lot, but she convinced herself that she had only been one client in a busy business and would not be missed, so that option seemed less hurtful to him.

She continued to wonder about his life, but in respect for his privacy, she did not try to find out. The memory of him running from her was still fresh. She would not want to become a nuisance in his life, or worse – a person he would want to avoid! Yes, leaving now would be best.

Then, she would have another dream.

Lingering feelings overlapped into her daily life. All she had now were occasional uninvited dreams where their souls could meet with awakened memories to experience complete unconditional love and peace of being together again. In fact, he continued in her dreams nightly, always at her side no matter what she was doing, or she was at his side no matter what he was doing. And that, from day to day, was an aching reminder of lost love.

The storyteller went silent for a while, lost in thought.

I eventually asked, "Is that the end of the story?"

"No. I could never figure out how to get beyond his professionalism to at least become friends. I crave to know him and hear stories about his life. I want to ask like a little kid, "Will you be my friend?" But I am afraid of looking like I've lost my marbles and most of all, being rejected again.

"Look at my story logically. Up until the day I humiliated myself in the parking lot, everything truly happened. I did have a real situation where I lost my shell and there was nothing protecting me from just spilling my guts out emotionally. I was suddenly living in a world of raw and unconditional love.

"Everything I believed about my life to that point was opened for inspection. I had a look into my own life to that point and accepted a few realities that I had swept under the rug, refusing to dwell on them. I had a habit of just picking myself up and being optimistic. I'm still really like that.

I need to pick myself up now. It's just a little harder this time.

"I did have an awakening memory that unseated my integrity and caused me to expect the unexpected in a world of rules about people. What happened beyond the day in the parking lot was my fantasy, a giant fantasy.

"You know, ironically, over the years I have known couples who married and lived happily without divorce even though the female was ten and even twenty years older than the male. Usually it's the other way around and more acceptable in society. These couples tended to be professional people who were able to adjust themselves in their work, have ongoing family relationships, shared children of their own relationship and of other marriages, and managed to keep their relationships growing. They should be writing a book. We should not judge odd relationships. We don't know what they have together or why.

"The odd thing is that in this physical world, I may be older than him but around him, I feel a lot younger than him. I do know that in a past life, he helped a great many people escape harm through an underground passageway. I recognize him as a brave, great man. I want to touch his feet and worship the ground he walks on. What does that say about time and reality? We are more than our physical bodies ... a lot more.

"There is a moral to my story. I came to my senses one day. I realized that interfering in another person's life, even in dreaming, is unfair. No one should interfere with another person's freedom. If in future we do become friends, then, at least, I will know he has come of his own free will.

"This is the end of the story ... except that I will remember him forever ... and if I dream of him now, I accept it as a gift.

"Actually, I did have a dream just the other night. He was sitting on a chair at the side of a room, watching me provide food from a buffet to a group of children. There was an abundance of food even after the children had taken theirs. I looked over at him and realized he must be hungry, so I offered him food. He accepted. As he walked toward the food, I received a message and a vision from an unknown intelligence. In other words, I had a vision within a dream, that his present home life is not good for him. In the vision, he appeared darker skinned than he is and he appeared as a boy, aged ten or twelve, holding a blanket in tatters. I was being told by the unknown intelligence that he needs a safe place to sleep and a new blanket. I was eager to offer everything he needs.

"Now, when I no longer ask, dreamland is telling me that he is in need of my loving care. If this is true or not, I have no way of knowing. He is silent, but he is still in most of my dreams.

"There is a reason for having amnesia between incarnations. It is protection so that most humans never have to question their lifetimes. Remembering can be wonderful but painful. I have no solution for myself. If I see him, I love him all the more each and every time I see him and I miss him more. If I don't see him, I miss him like losing part of myself. For me, it is difficult either way. I've played a joke on myself because I never wanted to do this. I can't get over him. I've tried. I've even prayed to get over him. That should be a song.

You know, one of those songs about love and desire. Maybe something like this ...

> The sun does shine
> in a new dawn after each sunset.
> She romps in grasses
> laced with wild flowers
> while waiting for him,
> a beloved dream
> that lives outside of time

"It doesn't rhyme. Anyway, it should be a story for your book.

"My life has an empty space without him. But unconditional love means that I truly want only the best for him, even without me. I pray that he is well taken care of ... And maybe in times of need, his soul knows I love him ... "

Writer's note:
In a timeless zone, they had no beginning and no ending. They had become just another story about love, sex, desire, a lost lover, and the wrath of a storm of emotions.

Just another Story

THE JOURNEY

bohemian coffeehouse

As I stood in my living room, I could feel that my husband was being unfaithful to me with the waitress. I had just finished playing with my children and putting them to bed. After working at my secretarial job all week, I was supposed to go to our coffee house and read cards on Friday evenings when folk music would be on stage.

I was looking at a life-size oil painting on my dimly lit living room wall. I had painted the portrait of Eric and myself in a moment of hopefulness and to celebrate his gift of oil paints. I was thinking that being intuitive is not an easy way to live because energy cannot be hidden; people seem to think they can do secret things, but energy is universal.

I went to the kitchen and grabbed a large sharp knife. Then I took the painting off the wall and slit it down the middle, separating the two figures to symbolically tell myself I had enough!

I put on my coat and boots and carried the damaged painting through the cold evening to the coffeehouse. Each step I took sounded crunches of snow and ice beneath my feet. The cold air felt good on my hot face. I did not really know what I was going to do, but I was angry enough to throw the slashed painting at Eric in front of everyone to make a point that we were finished.

A mellow song drifted to my ears through the dim light of candles on red and white tablecloths and the smoky air. My eyes followed the sound and found the guitarist up on the tiny stage at the other end of the crowded room. I slowly realized he was singing to me. He was telling me in song about his need to find his fortune by going away from here to New York. He wanted to know if I would read his cards and tell him his fortune.

Faces, mostly familiar university students, were turned my way in anticipation of my answer and then their eyes fell on the large canvas. Realizing that some of those faces also knew of my personal problems was humiliating. I stood there with my slashed painting, now feeling vulnerable and small. The steam had left me. Eric was not there to throw anything at anyway. Someone came forward and took the canvas from me, making it disappear.

My heart hurt. I needed to keep face. Looking after someone in need would help. I sat at my table and waved my serenader over.

He shuffled the cards and I laid them out. Three times. Yes, he must go find fame and fortune in New York.

When the reading was done, the waiter came to me and mumbled, "Someone has stolen all the till money tonight."

"Where's Eric?" I demanded.

"I don't know," he shrugged.

"Did he leave with Joanne?"

"Yes. I've been alone. I couldn't serve people and guard the till at the same time."

Money was gone from the till. I could not have cared less. I walked out – fast.

Cold prairie air slapped my face, waking me to my senses. My breath was hot steam in the air. I became aware of the strangely soothing rhythmic crunch of dry snow beneath my boots. My pace slowed. By the time I reached home, calmness was about me.

Dismissing my babysitter, I looked in on each of my sleeping children. Each one was special and though very small, they were so grown up in their own way. Tousled curls topped each head. I could still hear their voices as we had all frolicked together before they went to sleep. We had been so happy.

What would we all do now? What do little children do when families break up? Oh, God, not my children. I don't want my children to suffer. My oldest son was only eight and the next son was only six. My daughter was three. How would they understand?

My room was dimly lit with light coming only from the hallway through the open doorway. I lay on my side of the bed, avoiding the emptiness of my husband's side. Life just seemed too troublesome sometime. I wanted to sleep and have some relief. I lay there looking at the ceiling, listening to minutes tick away by the old clock on the dresser. Everything was quiet. The world was quiet except for the old clock and my unfaithful husband.

Suddenly, I began to rock. My body was not moving but my whole being was rocking from side to side on the inside of my body. With a whoosh, I smoothly slid upward through my head, out of my body.

Astonished, I paused and looked to see what had happened. I was definitely out of my body, hovering near my head – just above. Even though my head was near the wall, there was no wall. I had free range. I was definitely intact. I was all there.

All my senses were in fact more sensitive. I could see, hear, smell, feel, taste, but more than that, I could hear and see with a special sense. I did not need my eyes to see or my ears to hear or my skin to feel. It was like impressions upon me were all I needed. I had a more profound sense of 'knowing' than my own body had ever known.

I could see my silver cord fastened from me to my body. It really is true! I really have a silver cord!

My body was lying there below me and I was also aware of how it was feeling. It was comfortable lying there with me out here. My body's skin could feel every single thread of the upper and lower sheets, and even the weave of the threads. The sensitivity of my body magnified thousands of time the feeling of its surroundings.

Deciding that my body was safe and that I was just fine in this out-of-body state, I began to move out farther.

It was quite dark as I traveled a pathway that was like a tunnel. I became aware of other beings watching me from along the sides. They started moving closer. Some were calling to me, beckoning me to stop. I could see and hear them with my special senses. They were round, dimly lit beings with what seemed to me dimly developed senses. They were reaching out to me, wanting help. I paused. I could hear them begging for me to stay and help them. Realizing that it was wrong for me to stay in this place and that I might get sapped of energy here, I moved on, closing out their pleadings.

The path I traveled became lighter as I slowly made my way through the beings and left them behind.

I could see light and as I moved closer to it, I saw a city – a great city in the sky. Where? I did not know. But it was as real as anything I had ever known to be real. Moving closer, I came to the city's edge. I looked in at all the bright lights and knew a great many beings lived there.

I rested there and just looked and contemplated what was before me.

Suddenly fear hit me. What was I doing? What was I doing here? What if I lost my way? The silver cord snapped me back into my body.

I lay there wide-eyed, knowing I had not been sleeping nor did I dream or imagine what happened. This was for real. I tested my body. I was for sure back in my body and as normal as ever. I contemplated what had just happened and where I had just been. I knew this was going to be with me forever. Also, I knew life on earth for me would never be the same again, since I knew for sure there is life beyond this earth.

I thought back to my childhood. I had done this before, many times. This was not a new experience.

Wide eyed, the time ticked away. My children slept soundly in the next room.

Downstairs the door opened. My eyes flew to the clock that said three-thirty in the morning. I pretended to be sleeping as my husband crept upstairs to the bathroom. I could hear the water running, and running, as he was obviously trying to scrub his body clean. I pretended to sleep as he came to bed.

In the morning, studying myself in the bathroom mirror, I looked for clues of why my husband was unfaithful. This had not been the first time. I knew that. Why was this time worse than all the others? Why? I reasoned that it was because this time I knew other people also knew. I hurt. My face? Not unattractive. Each of my features was correctly in place. My body? I enjoyed my healthy elastic body, inside and out. No matter how many times I thought my body would explode with a pregnancy, like magic it always sprung back into its original form. I had good genes. I had a zest for life and a sense of humor. I could see nothing unattractive.

On the other hand, I analyzed him for a minute. He had a history of being unfaithful to his former wife long before I met him. I thought back to him hiding in the bathroom when it was time for bed because he had a hard time keeping up with my libido. Then, to prove himself to himself, he went after conquests like an animal on the prowl.

As I gazed into my mirror, I decided that his warped problems were not mine. I was only dealing with his reflection on me, except that I was feeling cheated of love. But, I had enough. His behavior could impact my health and that was what I needed to deal with once and for all.

Carefully, I ran a yellow ribbon around my head and tied it. I liked wearing ribbons. Lipstick on my lips and I was ready to face the world, or was I?

Eric met me at the door of the bathroom. He had just woken up. I backed into the room and let him come in with me. Closing the door so that no little ears could hear us, I confronted him.

"You were with a woman last night, weren't you?"

Being caught showed in his eyes as they shifted, looking for escape. Resting his eyes on the sink where he had scrubbed last night, he said, "Yes."

"That waitress."

"... Yes."

"How could you? She's my hired help. I pay her wages. Not only that, but I work as a secretary all week to keep paying for everything, the coffeehouse, our rent for this house, and babysitters for looking after the children so that I can work to pay for everything. Meanwhile you screw around at leisure ... not only the waitress, but any woman I make friends with and my babysitters while I am at work. I found a bra stuffed in my laundry basket just last week that was not mine. I know who it belongs to. I know she ran out the back door in a hurry when I came through the front door and you had to ditch the bra."

I had no idea how to put into words everything that hurt me and how I felt used.

He stood there waiting for whatever came next. I looked for what could be attractive about him to other women. He was tall, dark curls, and olive complexion. He did have lively brown eyes and a gleaming smile that had caused me to overlook other flaws in the beginning and supposedly could attract other women. Inner beauty was missing. He was a liar. I could no longer have any female fiends. I felt my life was being compromised.

I turned and quickly left the bathroom. I put on my coat and boots. Dashing out of the house, I could hear the children upstairs. I needed to think.

Several times around the park in the freezing weather and I knew suicide could never be my answer. He was not worth dying for. My children were worth living for. My children! I must go home!

"Forgive me." Eric was begging, "I will never do it again."

Contemplating my hurt, I looked at him long and hard. The silence seemed too much for him.

"You must forgive me for your own soul. You shouldn't harbor anything unworthy of you. Be free and forgive me."

Forgive him! How dare he talk about my soul! What about his?

I yelled, "What about your lousy cheating soul?"

"Let me worry about my soul but don't let this wreck your life and the lives of our children."

Our children? Yes. I must think of innocent children.

"Alright, but I can't go on like this. You have to be faithful from now on no matter what or we must separate. Why have you been unfaithful? That waitress – you know she screws anything that walks. Why would you jeopardize our lives for that?"

"I don't know. She doesn't mean anything to me. She's just a poor kid who can't light a candle to you."

"Then, why?"

"You're so right – so morally right. You're a mother, so pure. What more can I say? She's so trampy, but so excitingly trampy. I feel sorry for her trampyness."

"Ugh! You make me feel sick."

"Don't. Don't let this jeopardize the family. I'll be faithful from now on."

"How can I go on? How can I face everyone now?" I wailed.

"You can," he was condescending now.

I wished what had happened could be removed rather than having to deal with it. Perhaps he was right. I did not want to harbor bad feelings.

Just to make sure I would not leave, that evening he invited several men who had watched me crash and burn in the coffeehouse, to the house. As we sat around the fireplace, the men tried to convince me that Eric's relationship with the waitress meant nothing and I was not supposed to be upset. I was thinking they were all a bit nuts and certainly they were not my friends.

Loyalty had long ago replaced any thoughts of romance or even love. This was a second marriage for both of us and I knew it should end now. I felt like I was offering myself as a sacrificial lamb because of loyalty to what I had started.

the move

The old oak wood gleamed softly. I watched my dining room suite being carried out of the house. Table, buffet, china cabinet, then chairs went by me one by one. Alternating between rage and saintliness, memories overlapped the scene – family dinners, dinners with guests, but most of all the memory of what this dining room suite represented. Eric had given it to me as a symbol of his love for me. It was second-hand so it meant that all the generations before us would blend with our present and future generations to eat at this table.

Eric had convinced me that to prove my wonderfulness, my forgiveness, I must put my soul on display and give this dining room suite to the waitress he had slept with. The world would see my pure soul.

How could I have said yes? My head reeled. I could stop it now. Why couldn't I? I hated Eric at that moment as I realized what he was doing. Why didn't I just stop it? But in a way it did not matter. Yes, she would never forget me now but we were going on to a new life. Ironically, because of being coerced to make a gift of my furniture to her, we were tied by energy to ensure I would never forget her.

He wanted to leave town and start over in another city. We would give everything away and sell the coffeehouse. I was yet to realize that in my so-called saintliness, I would never collect on the sale. In time, it would be simply forgiven, too.

During the next few days, I watched my grandfather's bed leave along with my mother's armoire and all the beautiful things I had gathered over the years – all the memories going with them, until we were down to clothing, a few dishes, and bedding.

As we drove out of town, children in the back seat of the car with our only worldly belongings on the roof and stuffed into the trunk, I realized the impact of what was happening. We were leaving family and family roots. Children were losing grandparents and grandparents were going to know loneliness. No more would they hear the daily laughter of their grandchildren. I would lose companionship of sisters. No more would we have large family Sunday dinners at my parent's home.

We were causing all this to happen because Eric was running away from his unfaithfulness. Sadness permeated the trip.

Along the trip, while traveling through forest by Lake Superior, I had a strong knowledge so tangible, so certain that I shuddered. I knew that I did not want to grow old with this man, and for sure, I never wanted to live with him in this kind of wilderness. I did not want to be alone with him. Unknown to me then, I was having real foreknowledge of the future because later in life he would return to live in this exact area. I would not be with him.

golden eagle

I had a dream. A golden eagle was washing me in a stream of clear water. The lucid dream was brilliant and stayed in my mind. I knew something new and different was about to happen to my life.

new start

In a tent on a beach along the way, I had become pregnant.

Now in the big city, six month pregnant and sitting cross-legged on the gleaming wood floor with ten other people, I was filled with anticipation of what this great man would say. Just that day, I had received a telephone call that a Buddhist monk would be in town and if Eric and I wanted to meet him, we could.

Well, we were here and a real live Buddhist monk sat facing us at the other end of the room. He was dressed in saffron colored robes and held sandalwood beads. On his head, he wore a rather conical shaped hat with flaps down over the sides of his neck. His eyes were closed. The stillness of his body permeated the room.

Minutes passed by, seeming to grow longer. Some of the people present were also sitting with eyes closed. The uneven breathing and odd clearing of throats gave them away.

I had never meditated before, so I thought over the events bringing me here. I had studied the occult, reading cards, palm reading, and even tried the Ouija Board. Alan Watts had taught me a little about Zen thought through his writing and one of his lectures that I attended.

Lost in reverie, I was startled back into the room when the monk stirred. He opened his eyes and looked at each of us as he moved his robes a little here and a little there.

There was another long pause. Then he spoke softly.

"Welcome. You have come to learn. You will learn. You have come to see. You will see."

There was another pause. We all seemed to sit on the edge of our bums.

"First," he went on, "let me set some of you straight. We do not use what you will learn for selfish reason. Remember that. I will use many devious methods to teach you and you will learn, despite yourselves. I will teach by the left-handed Tantra where necessary. But, we do not resort to such lowly devises as séances and Ouija Boards. We do not read cards here. None of that."

My God, I thought. Is he talking to me? I could not believe my ears. Surely no one had gone to the trouble of telling him about me. I felt very uneasy and defensive. I certainly knew of nothing wrong with what I did. And what was this left-handed Tantra? It sounded scary. My indignant daydream was interrupted in the realization that he had gone on.

"You will prepare yourself for life after life. There is no death. Your present delusion is your flesh and bones, your ties which are all delusions. You belong to no one and no one belongs to you. You cannot own another person."

I was having real trouble with this. You bet I owned my husband and children and they had better own me. This was making me downright uneasy.

"You must clear your minds and you will clear your lives. You must meditate. You will meditate. That is the way. You cannot do any clearing by filling yourself with intellectual discussion of the scriptures. We will do some intellectual study but we will meditate."

There was another pause. He looked long at each of us. I tried to hide my mind as he gazed at me.

"I will see each one of you privately. You will make appointments with me. Now I will teach you all to meditate."

He then taught us a simple meditation.

remembering a spirit

Later, Eric was delighted and acted as though he had finally found what he had been looking for. His interpretations of the discourse spelled trouble to my ears. He had found someone to tell him he could be a free man. Trying to convince me of his point of view was useless.

That night in bed, a profound chord was struck within me. I remembered back to when I was about two years of age. I would lie in bed beside my father. My mother would be in the kitchen. My father would be reading to me. I would always lie with one leg under the blankets and one over the blankets while listening to my father's voice and trying to see what he was reading. A man would suddenly appear night after night. He would stand very still and silently inside the doorway in front of an armoire and look at me. His very intent brown eyes would look deeply into my eyes. I would immediately feel uneasy, put my uncovered leg inside and cover up to my neck. He was always dressed in long red clothes and a red hat. Now I realized they were saffron robes and hat just as I had seen tonight. A lump seemed to settle in my chest now.

As a child, I had told my parents about this man appearing each night and we moved from the house because of him. I was not aware of seeing him after that, but the memory of him, especially his eyes, remained vivid all my life.

private meeting

It was only a few days later that I found myself again sitting with the Buddhist monk who was now known to all of us as the Bhikhu. We understood that name to mean 'teacher', although the dictionary meaning is 'fully ordained monk'.

My intention had been never to see him again but as though by magnetism, I had to see him. This was my private session and I intended to confront him about my viewpoints.

He smiled a slow, soft smile that penetrated my intense ego. I softened. Was I giving up before I began?

Trying to impress him, I told him about my most recent astral travel experience, and actually, I had never told anyone else. I was telling him my secret. Expecting praise for my accomplishment, I was taken back by these words.

"You must know how to control what you do. Anything done without control is dangerous. It is no more than an accident. You must learn control."

Staring into his eyes, I felt my astonishment and ignorance showing. We sat in silence for a while. He was in no hurry. It was as though the world had slowed down in this room.

Breaking the silence, my voice sounded too loud. "Did someone tell you I read cards and all those things?"

"No. No one told me."

"What... What... Why did you mention those things?"

"Be aware and you will understand. I do not need to be told many things. Intuition is you as a receiving instrument. Intuition is your guidance. Thoughts vibrate eternally in the cosmos. You are a sender and a receiver. We all are. Most people live deaf and blind even though they have ears and eyes. They are not open to the fine-tuning. We are like radios sending and receiving. Most people become indignant out of fear. What they do not see and hear or touch, they believe to be invalid. When all they have to do is open their minds, listen with their inner being – their true selves, and see beyond their nose. What is outside is inside. What is inside is outside. Look to nature for the secrets of the universe."

Assimilating this took a while. We again sat in silence.

"I read cards." My voice was small now. "I do all those things – cards, palms. We've had some interesting sessions."

His eyes steadfastly looked into mine. "What have you learned by it? Has it made you happy?"

This question cause me to blurt out, "No! No! It's like hitting my head against the wall over and over again. I keep looking for answers but only get more questions. It's awful. It makes me unhappy. It feels dark in there. There are no answers. And really, it makes my mind hurt, wanting answers and not getting them. It's so frustrating."

I knew I'd been unhappy doing this, but this torrent of disillusionment exasperated my ego. I sat there examining my answer.

"You are ready for more," he counseled. "You must meditate."

There was another long pause.

With twinkling eyes now, he asked, "Will you be our coordinator of the Meditation Centre?"

This was certainly unexpected by me. I had come here expecting to go away disappointed and here

I was being drawn in completely. I loved this guru with all my heart right then.

"Yes. Yes. But what meditation centre?"

"We will have one and there will be many Buddhist monks and nuns. There will be hundreds of people meditating. You shall see."

"When?"

"Very soon. This is January. ... I think by March."

"March ... uh, what about my family? I have children."

"Children will be good for the meditators. Children will keep them on their toes. They will not lose their way so easily."

What a strange thing to say, I thought. "I agree. Anyway that's my thinking. Children are where it's at."

Solemnly he went on, "Your job will not be easy. You will live in poverty. You will give of yourself in service of others."

"I know." I sounded confident.

learning to meditate

Learning to meditate turned out to be a self-analysis process that required control. Persistence in the face of self-destruction in the process was a constant battle in the beginning.

I thought that we would be so inclined toward peace and understanding that it would be easy to sit there meditating, feeling great, and taking a rest from responsibilities. Not me. The first step is overcoming body itches. Aspiring meditators develop itches on legs, arms, anywhere and everywhere on the body – ears, nose, head, intended to drive one out of trying to meditate. The first lesson is to ignore these itches and they would go away. Aches! With itches gone, the aches developed. Then came the twitching. I had them all.

Meanwhile, the mind that I thought was in my control was running rampant. My thoughts, I discovered, controlled my emotions and me. Controlling my mind was one of the most difficult tasks I could ever undertake.

"You will turn inside out." Bhikhu counseled. "You will find the secret of the universe within yourself. What is inside is outside. What is outside is inside. It is all the same."

I had gotten past body interruptions. Now I had a bigger struggle.

"When you find your mind wandering, start over. Do not continue. Start over until you master your thoughts. You must learn to control your mind or it will wander unfettered, ruling you. Control. Train your mind."

I struggled to control my thoughts. How my mind wandered. I had never realized how totally out of control my mind had been. It conjured up people's faces and actions taking place before my eyes. Conversations took place in my head. Problems of relationships, problems of daily living, responsibilities all refused to let me get on with what I expected would be peace.

"Learn control by watching. Observe how your mind works, then you will learn control." Bhikhu's voice penetrated my thoughts. Was I the only one of his students having problems? We all were. His discourse last evening had been on 'observing' one's self in meditation but also every minute of the day.

This was proving interesting and more difficult than it sounded. Just when my conscious mind seemed to be in my control, images and thoughts drifted up from the depth of me. My subconscious mind was hard at work.

"You must learn to control your thoughts, your actions and your speech. You must cut through your ego. This is all delusion. Your egos think it is all real. Your egos keep you from knowing what is real.

"Why suffer any longer. You can do it ... you can know complete awareness."

Just when I thought I was learning control of my thoughts, my actions and speech had to be controlled. Speech proved to be my problem. My actions were easy to control but my mouth continued to protect my interests.

"You must use your powers with discrimination. If you use power selfishly or to destroy others, your power will turn on you and destroy you," Bhikhu taught.

He pulled out a deck of Tarot cards. Holding up the thirteenth Arcana card, Death, his vice boomed. "You must know this card, understand the meaning of this card. At first glance this looks like death in the form of a skeleton wielding a scythe. Death and destruction. Look closer. This is destruction followed by change. There is new growth below his feet. As he reaps, new growth appears. Transformation – renewal – rebirth. This card does not mean death; it means change, regeneration of the soul and eternal life. The number thirteen is not unlucky. It is a number that will destroy the user if it is used selfishly. If used unselfishly, it brings new life."

Now, he held up the Fool card. "Most of you are now like the Fool. You are stepping off the edge of the cliff, looking upward, unaware of what is beneath your feet. You carry your stored up universal knowledge on the end of a stick, loftily over a shoulder. Some of you might use it like a chip on your shoulder to prove your wisdom to others."

Leaning forward, he cautioned in a lowered voice, "Be careful."

Then he sat straight again and went on, "You know not what you are getting into. The Fool is youthful innocence about to enter a supreme adventure."

He sat looking at each of us; then told us, "You must keep your feet on the ground even though your head is in the clouds. Balance. You must keep balance."

meditation centre

The meditation centre did come into being at the end of March. I also gave birth to my fourth child on the last day of March.

Acres of fields and groves of trees, streams and a tiny lake, all picture book beautiful, had been purchased. To be one of a group of people to found this mediation centre was something to be proud of.

The old log house with floors you could fall through and gaping cracks in the walls, had to be fixed. The house was large with two upstairs bedrooms. The main room was enormous and would have multipurpose use. The kitchen was big enough to cook for many people with room enough to seat them around a big table.

I wandered around, trying to visualize being at home here with my family. There was no electricity, no washing machine, nothing but wood fires, no running water. What was I getting into?

I was among the first few people to visit the centre. My husband had been told by the Bhikhu to stay home and baby-sit. What a blow to his ego that had been! He had been bragging about his new life out here as though he had been chosen top man of the meditation group but I was sent out to the centre while he babysat. I thought it quite a trick played on him by his guru.

Outside, I sat on a hill, meditating. Clean air. Sunshine. It felt so good ... so cleansing. I opened my eyes as I could hear others approaching.

Something opposite of what I was enjoying suddenly seemed to settle around me. It was as though a dark shadow had emerged out of a crack. I had only a glimmer of it and could not exactly see the dark shadow. A foreboding came over me. Deja vu? But what? It was familiar. Had I dreamed the event? Yes, I had seen this place in a dream. Now I knew that. Yes, I knew long ago that I would live here ... years before. Only now had I remembered. But what else? What was going to happen here? The more I tried to remember, to plead with my brain to remember, the more it closed down.

Picking grass and running green ribbons through my fingertips, I knew this was some kind of destiny and I was merely following through.

work at the centre

Eric was never one to be outdone by me. He was leaving on a work trip to the meditation centre. I had been told he would be going with other men. Seeing him to the door with my daughter by my side, we cheerfully hugged and kissed when I saw that a woman was waiting for Eric in the back seat of the car. They were going with a married couple that was also among our founding members. They would be two men and two women. I suddenly realized that I thought these people were my friends, but behind my back they were complicit with Eric's adultery. Dumbstruck, the knowledge of what was happening made me speechless.

Before I could say anything, Eric ran to the car. Panic came over me as he rode off in the back seat beside Mary who had been flirting outrageously with him at our meditation meetings.

It was hard for me to imagine Eric with Mary, but I just saw it with my own eyes. She was a darkly, sullen person with burning, tortured, black eyes that usually tore into my skin with jealousy. She repelled me. I always felt that she would harm me and my children and that had been borne out when we found ourselves in an art therapy group run by a woman sculptor, another founding member. We were in the sculptor's dead husband's art studio. Mary was at another table pouring black paint and fiercely scrubbing the paint across her paper while aggressively looking at me. Her intention was evident; she was directing bad energy at me. I pretended not to notice and continued painting.

I could not go on work weekend trips because of the children and especially because I had a new baby. Eric had a perfect way out.

I was a new mother with raging hormones of nesting and of wanting to be loved and cared for. My weekend was miserable. My pride fought with humility until I finally called Bhikhu and told him what was happening.

"Do not be concerned," he told me over the telephone. "That is Eric's karma, not yours."

"But my marriage, my family,"

There was sadness coming through his voice and I wondered if there was a touch of worry, but I could not get a rise out of him.

When Eric returned, he denied any wrongdoing.

He tried to reassure me, "Sure, we slept in the same tent but we were in separate sleeping bags,"

"You must think I'm a child to believe you slept separately in the same tent."

Dismissing my concerns was his only concern. "Soon you'll be living there and she won't. We'll be happy. You'll see."

I was beyond showing emotional needs or distress to him. I had gotten good at smothering hurt feelings. As usual, I went on ignoring our problems as much as possible. Eric went to live on the centre for three weeks during which time we were totally separate. We had given up our house in the city. While waiting for my house in the country to be ready, I visited my family in another province. This arrangement suited Eric very well. In fact, he wanted to delay our return indefinitely.

home sweet home

Arriving back on a brilliant summer day, I was disappointed that Eric was not greeting us at the train station. Bhikhu had sent his two main students who were his long-time helpers to pick us up and drive us to the meditation centre. On arrival at the meditation centre, Eric hardly acknowledged our return. Instead, he continued whatever he was working on with Mary keeping watch over him.

Home, sweet home. Or would it be? I needed time to settle in and unpack. My children needed to play and get to know their new home. Instead, there were a lot of other people around. I had unknowingly arrived when there was a week of meditation going on.

In excitement, the children romped around the house and called to each other from different rooms.

An excited lady appeared at the kitchen door. "SSshh—ss," her lips were screwed up and she frowned.

"What's the matter," I asked.

"There are meditators out there in tents. You'll disturb them."

My heart sank. This was just the beginning. The feeling of uptightness and restriction, worse than we had known, was here and now. My boys' faces looked strained already and mine was worse.

In walked Bhikhu. "Welcome. I'm glad you made it," his voice boomed and seemed to carry out the windows and doors, and over the hills. "Hi, kids."

He grabbed one and swung him around, tousled the hair of another, lifted my daughter into his arms and shook the hand of my eldest. Before long there was a minor wrestling match going on with my children on one team and Bhikhu as their opponent. He was quick in movement and soon had all three pinned, hollering for help. His agility was different than I had ever seen. My sons wanted to know how he had managed to throw them with a flick of a finger.

"Aikido." His eyes twinkled. "Want to learn some Aikido?" he asked the boys.

With Aikido lessons already in progress, it was plain the meditators would have to put up with us, noise and all.

the log house

New flooring had been laid and the kitchen stove put it. My large table was in the centre of the room. At the far wall stood a wood-burning cooking stove bought from the nearest neighbor who had painted a large colorful lion on the backsplash above my cook-top. I fell in love with the stove and the lion right away. Much to my surprise, minimal electricity had been strung – just one line, enough for my refrigerator that came from the city, and a light bulb in each room on the main floor. The house was fixed enough to live in right now and I immediately felt right at home in my domain, the kitchen.

Understanding that people were anxious to use the place was easy. After all, they owned it. I wished there had been time for us to be alone here to be at home for while, be a family, to talk to Eric. Instead, we were thrust into a meditation weekend head on. I would have to find my way on my own with a pretend partner. The group of people had grown by leaps and bounds the last few weeks, nearing fifty people now. Word had gotten around fast.

food problems

Bhikhu had gone out so that the children and I could get our bearings, and he had other things to do.

A car drove up.

"Here are the groceries." A little, old man came in carrying a cardboard box full of food.

Three boxes later, he turned to me and said, "I've worked out the menu. It's over there on the cupboard."

I had been watching in dismay. Now I was puzzled.

I asked, "How long is this food to last and for how many people?"

"Thirty people. They'll be here all week."

"Thirty people? All week? Uh...oh, three boxes?" My fingers pointed toward the boxes.

He answered, "Oh, I've worked it all out. The menu is on the counter." He sounded confident but I could have been blown away.

Peeking into the boxes, it was totally unreasonable to me that these boxes should feed thirty people for a week. My kids alone could devour it all, except that they would hate most of it.

I read the menu. He certainly had worked it all out. Every meal, three each day, carefully recorded for a whole week. But thirty people? They would have to eat like birds! Right! That's it! His wife and he looked extremely emaciated. They should not expect us all to eat like they did. Necessary snack foods for my children – there would be absolutely none.

The meditators were all in tents strewn over the acreage. Bhikhu was also somewhere out there. I stood outside my house and rocked my baby in my arms while wondering how to do what I needed to do and look after my children. Just when I needed someone to help me, a light-haired, middle-aged woman appeared suddenly beside me. I had never seen her before and after this afternoon I would never see her again. She offered to look after my baby for me and carefully took my baby into her arms. I immediately trusted her. I told her I needed to leave all the children with her for a short while and I went searching for Bhikhu, determined to get a few things straight.

Up on a hill was a rather large orange tent with a big, screened room off to the side. There he sat giving individual counsel to his students. I waited my turn at the bottom of the hill.

"Hi, I'm Peter." A young man turned to me and smiled. "You going to live here, huh?"

"Yes."

Just then the student in the tent came out, followed by Bhikhu who stood with his hands on his hips calling, "Peter, Peter, pumpkin eater, had a wife and couldn't keep her."

Peter headed up the hill and into the screened area where I could watch but not hear.

Minutes later, Peter came down the hill with a bewildered look on his face. As he passed by me, he muttered, shaking his head, "How did he know I have a letter in my pocket from my girlfriend – a letter saying goodbye?"

"You mean an ex-girlfriend?"

"You got it." Peter headed off into the woods.

My turn. Slightly nervous, I made my way up the hill. Inside the tent, the brilliant orange glow was jewel-like.

"What can I do for you?" He sat on a chair facing me and I took the edge of a chair, my sandaled feet planted squarely in the grass.

"The food. There's not enough. If I'm to cook, I want to also plan the menu. The menu ... it's not got enough protein. Some days, it's practically got none. I don't think that man knows what he's doing. I need to make my own menus."

The complaints rolled over my tongue. I had been at the centre for two hours and I was already complaining wildly. Feeling as though my soul had just been bared of a terrible sin, I anticipated an angry response. Never the less, feeling righteous about the whole matter, I went on.

"Those people are going to be starved after a week. Three small boxes of food, two pounds of cheese, two dozen eggs for more than thirty people ...... for a week!" My voice had risen and seemed to fall on the grass under my feet.

A glimmer of annoyance crossed Bhikhu's eyes. He spoke softly. "He needs to do that job. He's working out his karma."

"But how can I manage? He doesn't know how to do the job."

"I never said your job would be easy." With that he rose from his chair, walked to the zippered doorway, dismissing me.

Anger blazed through me as I walked down the hill. Heading for the woods, I felt like my children were being abandoned by me but I needed to be alone to think.

What on earth had possessed me to come here? Other people's karma! What about my own? What about my children, my marriage? Eric was ignoring me as best he could now with so many other people around. The woods were quiet and restful. New buds everywhere – new life. Kicking stones, I meandered along, head down, trying to make sense out of what I'd been told.

"Hey, what are you doing out here?" Eric was sauntering in his relaxed manner toward me, grinning.

"Thinking. What are you doing here?" I was surprised but wondered whose tent he had come from.

"Just looking over the dead wood for firewood." His arm swept the air around him. "Look," he pointed, "there's lots of old logs fallen. If we run out of that, there's plenty of wood in the stands to go on for years."

"But it won't last forever. What then?"

Somehow, the using up of trees always seemed to hurt my brain. I never could sort out how we could use the trees and expect to have them to maintain balance in nature on so small a property, or planet for that matter.

"Don't worry your head about those things," Eric answered. "Hey, while you're here, I'll show you the spring where we get the water. You know, there's no water in the well. It's dry."

"No water in the well? No. I didn't know. You mean we have to hall water?"

"That's right."

Picturing myself relying on Eric for water and knowing that meant I would be out of needed water, I turned my back to him so that he would not see what I was thinking.

"Hey," he pulled me around by the shoulders, "What's a little problem with water?" His eyes grinned, "Come on. I'll show you the spring."

I followed him through the woods along a narrow path. On the opposite edge of the property, we came to a tiny spring. It really was an underground spring that was bubbling up out of the earth into a small rock lined pool of crystal clear water. Excess water ran off in a tiny stream through the woods. It was beautiful.

"You can't find better water than this anywhere." Eric was bending over it, smiling proudly.

Looking at the spring was the first thing we had shared in a long time. Looking into his face, mixed feelings welled up. I wanted to share life, love, and be young with someone, not just to be responsible and separate. I wished for real love.

snacks and salt eggs

Breathing a sigh of relief after dinner, I served tea. Bhikhu complimented me for the dinner and thanked me. Then he disappeared into the dusky evening.

It had been a long day. The children and I arranged the upstairs bedrooms for sleeping. It was pretty up there. The raw wood logs gave a warm glow in the candlelight. Well, at least we would be cozy up here, hidden away in our private family space.

The children were sleeping. I was alone in the kitchen, puttering around after washing dishes and cleaning up. Footsteps approached. The door opened and there stood Bhikhu.

"Well, what's for a bedtime snack?" he asked with a mischievous light in his eyes.

"A snack?" This was a total surprise to me, considering that I had explained the food situation to him just that afternoon.

While taking a chair by the side-table near the door, he said, "I think some of that cheese with bread and tea would do just fine."

He waited expectantly.

"Oh, yes. Sure. Uh, I'll get it."

He asked me about the children, advising me to care for them first. "Feed them well," he said, "They are growing boys and girls. They need nourishment."

I served the cheese and bread. I continued my work as he ate and drank tea, talking small talk.

"What's for breakfast?" he asked, looking at me with child-like innocence written across his face.

I reached for the menu. "Uh-h ... he says ..."

Bhikhu interrupted, "I'm homesick for a good breakfast of salt eggs and saffron rice."

"Salt eggs and saffron rice? Oh, I don't think that's written here at all. I don't even know how to make it."

"I'll show you." He got up, asking for the eggs and brown rice.

Together we boiled the eggs and peeled them. Laying them in the salt brine, he told me, "They'll be ready by morning. A good Tai breakfast. Now in the morning we will make the rice. I'll be here at 6:30."

He went out into the night, leaving me with a lot to think about. He had just boiled all the eggs in the house and put them in salt for breakfast. Those eggs would throw the menu off for the whole week. The menu was now useless. Of course, that's it! He was showing me how to deal with it all. I must accept the gracious help of the menu man, but I was to do what I must do to make my own job work and make my own life work. I did not have to be ruled by that other man.

Snacks! Right! My kids could have snacks and I was not to feel guilty about giving my own children special care. They are in my care and rely on me! How right!

From then on, the days were easier.

getting help

One week had gone by. I had now cooked meals for seven days. There were breakfasts, lunches and dinners for thirty guests and piles of dishes. I was constantly working. I was chief cook and bottle-washer, and main problem solver. No matter what the problem – from making sure there was enough food to baking bread, and making interesting meals to helping distraught meditators, I was depended upon. I marveled at people's ingenuity in dreaming up problems.

Bhikhu would come to the kitchen each evening after dark when all the meditators were back in their tents. He would play with the children, teaching the boys Aikido, laughing with them while they climbed over him. Each evening he would have a snack and talk.

Eric had been missing every evening but discovered Bhikhu's visits and joined in for a while.

Each evening, I knew we had been taught something more. Like little gems, Bhikhu would sprinkle his conversation with things meant for my ears.

The meditators went back to the city after that first week. From then on, there were often thirty or more guests on weekends. I never knew in advance how many guests would arrive. It was necessary to be ready for anything. Friday afternoon, rain or shine, they would all descend upon us again, staying until Sunday evening.

Eric had managed to retain help. He always seemed to have a sidekick to help him all week long while no one was willing to help in the kitchen.

Rumors of jealousy drifted back to me from the city about a few women who would like to take my place with Eric or wanted a favored place with Bhikhu.

Deciding to take matters into my own hands, I devised a plan that one weekend, I would be too busy to cook and wash dishes by myself. The next few weekends were work weekends anyway. The students were to come and build cabins and do maintenance to the acreage.

Friday night, I made a list of the female guests. I assigned jobs indoors to women who had shown jealousy of me. I wanted these women to see how hard I worked with no facilities and serving them on top of it each weekend. Mary, who had always stuck close to Eric, was on my list. I was determined to keep her indoors that weekend. When I assigned her the kitchen, she was furious.

Meanwhile, I set up my washtubs outside the house and proceeded to scrub clothes on my washboard. I carried water, heated it in large tubs over the stove, and then carried the hot water to the tubs outside and scrubbed all weekend.

Mutiny sprung up. Mary said she would not dirty her fingers in dishwater. Another woman said she had come with a plan to clean out a certain part of the woods and she wanted to know why I was interrupting her plan. On and on, they complained. Bhikhu had not come on this work weekend, so they had no one to complain to other than me. I was determined to teach them a lesson and ignored their grumbling.

The next weekend, I heard about it from Bhikhu. Every woman I had assigned an indoor job to, complained to him.

Seeing my hurt, he told me, "You should have help on weekends. I have told the student to give you help."

Help was offered on the following weekend – not from the same women though. I was not prepared for the kind of help I got. They would wash vegetables but the dirt would still be clinging. They would peel vegetables and only get part of the peels off. They would not wash their hands before handling food. The dishes were still greasy when put into the cupboard. I was embarrassed to serve some of the food that looked sloppy and dirty. Instructions from me found deaf ears. I was convinced that mothers everywhere had not taught their kids – these women in particular, anything about cleanliness. Their cooking ethics were carelessly dirty.

After a few cups of tea that tasted like soap and a few nights of washing dishes all over again, and a picnic lunch of dirty food served to Bhikhu, I gave up. Bhikhu had looked at me questioningly while eating politely. I now wanted to do the cooking and cleaning up all by myself. It would be easier.

Was I here to learn about my low tolerance of other people's capabilities, or was I here to learn tolerance of their lack of capabilities? Was I here to learn tolerance of other women? Maybe I was here to learn tolerance of our society in general. I did not know what to do with women who could not learn cleanliness. I did not know what to do with women who would wreck havoc on a home. Was I here to learn or teach? Enough is enough. I'd rather work alone.

Water had become a sore point between Eric and me. He never carried water unless he was on show for other people. When no one was around, I carried it or went without. Jealousy! Women were jealous of me? It beat me what for. I had to work darn hard to live here and what for? To serve? I was not even getting paid for my work. Free rent was all and nothing else. Feeding people who stayed on the meditation centre was costing me money from my personal life. Even my husband was fair game. I was gaining nothing. While I served others, I was neglecting my own children.

And women? I would not have long to wait to find out who my husband was now conquering. A young woman, someone I had befriended, brought a bag of her old clothes for me. I had few clothes, so I appreciated the rust colored corduroy slacks.

The next morning, I put them on and it was as though I was being burned with knowledge that whoever wore the pants had sex with my husband. I wore them down the stairs and when she came in for breakfast, I asked her if she did have sex with my husband. I was surprised when without hesitation, she said, "Yes."

I ask, "Where? When?"

She told me he would come to her tent when I thought he was working in the forest and she was supposedly meditating.

I had never worn secondhand clothing before this day. My lesson was to realize that wearing secondhand clothing was dangerous for me. I did not want to wear another person's life.

A sensitive person can pick up knowledge from objects, water, and through air because everything holds energy. Empty space of air is not empty.

seeing energy

Regardless of the problems with some women, I did have true friends in other women. A much older woman had been with Bhikhu for many years. He put her together with me right from the beginning; she became a friend and teacher to me.

I was on a walk with her and other women along the country road one night in the moonlight. I was looking upward at the millions of stars in the clear sky and marveling at the vastness of the universe. She told me to look at orgone energy in the air around me. It took me only a few seconds to see what she was talking about. I could see energy in the form of millions of light dots swirling and dancing in the air. A few moments ago it seemed to be empty space that I could feel but not see.

She had shown me the way to see life in the fabric of the universe.

Around this time, a blind man came to visit. He was a tall, white-haired, older man who walked with confidence and a white cane. He told me that by day, he had always been totally blind, but by night, he would astral travel and could see everything clearly. He told me he knew the color of everything. He was only with me for an afternoon, but he left me with a memory of a blind man who could see.

a burn

The wood stove turned out bread like I remembered from my mother and grandmother's wood stoves. Somehow, the bread tasted better than from an electric stove. I baked bread nearly every day. We basked in the smell.

Bhikhu was enjoying his Friday evening snack of fresh bread and sipping his tea.

I was busily sterilizing baby bottles. I would lift each one out of the boiling pot with my fingertips, carry it to the table where he sat and set it on a clean towel. I would return for another one and do the same routine. I could feel his eyes intently following my movements.

"Do you not burn yourself doing that?" he asked.

Turning to look at him, I laughed and jokingly answered, "Ha, when one is spiritual, one does not burn self."

"Oh," he mused. "Hmm, you think so?" His voice trailed off as he sipped tea again.

Saying goodnight, he left the house and I was left alone to finish my work. The fire needed more wood. I removed the lid of the stove and chose a piece of wood. Sliding it into the open flames, my hand slipped. My wrist came down onto the rim of the open hole. It was too hot. My skin sizzled. I could not believe my eyes. My wrist had a burn on it two inches wide, one inch long and it hurt. My earlier remark burned in my ears.

At breakfast, Bhikhu asked me, "What happened to your wrist?"

After my joke, my mishap was amusing me. I showed him my wrist.

He whispered to me, "Behind the illusions, dreams uncover the law. Time is our laboratory."

Now I had another gem of something to put into perspective – or, was he joking with me now?

the well

It was perfectly natural to me that my father was a water diviner. I grew up with the knowledge that many prairie farmers had functioning water wells that were dug with his advice on where to dig and how deep to dig for clean water. On several occasions, he took us children out onto the land with him to teach us how to divine water. He would cut just the right willow branches for each of us and we would walk slowly across the fields with him. I would hold my willow branch and marvel that it would dip and tug along side his branch. In my hands and arms, I could feel the strength of an unseen force working the twig. My father would explain the meaning of how deep, what color the water that ran through was, and which direction it flowed. He would comment that I had the gift and it should never be used for monetary gain because it was a gift. My father's teaching stuck in my mind and going after monetary gain never became my goal in life. Instead, I relished the gifts of life based on energy.

At the meditation centre, there was a picturesque stone well. When we first looked into the well in the beginning, it was dry and there were dead porcupines at the bottom. The well was cleaned but remained dry. Looking after my own family and hundreds of people coming and going without a reliable water supply was tough.

The only water source for drinking, cooking, and washing was the far away sparkling, pretty little stream that came out of the ground like a tiny fountain in the dense forest between some rocks on the land. To get water from the fountain meant a long walk hauling water in jugs or pails up and down the dirt road and over a large hill that ran alongside the land.

A man who visited only on weekends, watched me working in the kitchen. He then suggested a solution to water storage. He was able to get oak whisky barrels from the brewery he worked in. The next weekend, the barrels arrived and were filled with water from the stream and brought back by truck. Life seemed easier with two large oak barrels of water with real taps sitting in the kitchen.

Then came the weekend a few weeks later when several dozen hungry people arrived and I cooked their meals as usual. Then they left. I thought it had been a successful weekend until halfway through the next week a message reached me that many people had become ill. To my surprise, after working so hard on their behalf, I was being blamed for their illness. The rumor was that they thought I had probably cooked their meals with an improper frame of mind, causing illness. I knew this was not true and felt unjustly vilified by ungrateful people who had not bothered to help in any way, either by providing food or to help in the kitchen.

Bhikhu, approached me as I was busy cooking by the stove again on the next weekend. "Many people reported to me intestinal troubles after eating here last weekend. I told you to be free of aggression when you cook."

How dare he blame me! Indignation overcame me. Those people freeloaded every weekend and now were blaming my cooking. My face felt blazing hot.

Never one to back down to him, I turned to face him and glowered. "There is an old Chinese saying, 'If a thousand people say a foolish think, it is still foolish'."

With hands on hips I went on, "I say, if one person says a truth, it is still a truth. You can blame those blasted old moldy wine barrels for their gastric problems. And maybe you can blame their selfishness for tight asses and gastric problems." With that I stormed past him and out the door.

That evening, air was chilly. I stood shivering, looking into the well. Dry. Dry as could possibly be. Not even a drop of water. The stone walls had been scrubbed clean from top to bottom in hopes that it would fill up. No water.

"Please, well, I need water," I begged. "If you give me water, I'll plant flowers all around you."

Back at the house, I soon forgot the well as I had more guests to look after.

In the morning, pancakes were lined up on the stovetop. It held ten at a time and they had become my trademark. Breakfast guests were drifting in.

"Hey, the well's full of water,' I heard from a distance.

Could it be? I handed the spatula to another person and ran out.

Approaching the well, I could see that it had filled with water overnight. It had not rained, so this was some kind of miracle. In fact, it was so full of water that it was over the top and had a large pool of water on the ground surrounding the well so that no one could even get near the water in the well.

As darkness approached that evening, I went out to the well and stood as close as I could.

I spoke to the well. "Thank you, well. Thank you for all the water. But I cannot get near enough to use your water because there is too much. I need to have water this far from the top." I showed a measurement in the air with my hands of approximately two feet. I felt a presence as though I was really talking to a person.

I was in the habit of getting out of bed in the second floor of the house and going to the window to enjoy the countryside view in the morning light. The next morning I ran from my bed to the window to look out at the well. I was astonished to see that the water was still there. It was still true. Now I could see that the water was exactly, and I mean exactly, at the level of two feet from the top of the stone wall – just as I had asked.

I ran down the wooden staircase and out to the well. The ground around the well was dry.

Now I realized the water was still unusable because it looked dirty. It had dirt and leaves floating on top and all through as deep as I could see.

That very evening, alone again, I went back to the well.

"Thank you, well, for all the water and thank you for the right depth, but I need clean water. I need you to be clean enough to drink."

Again, there was a feeling of a presence other than myself.

In the morning sunshine, I stood by a well of water that sparkled with clean water. There was not a leaf or a spec of dirt in it. It was a perfect level and the ground was dry around it. The well had responded to me. I thanked the spirit of the water. I believed I was seeing with my own eyes, the tangible power of the unseen world.

The whole thing was unbelievable but the proof was right there in front of the other people. We had the water tested. It proved to be absolutely pure and clean. We used the well water from then on and I had no more problems with water during my time at the centre. There were no more complaints of intestinal upsets over my cooking.

There was just one minor problem. It soon became apparent that not just anyone could get water from the well.

The well was close to the house, so I felt I could ask nearly anyone to fetch a pail of water. The first time I tried this, the young fellow had gone out with the pail confidently, but came back white-faced with an empty pail. He told me that no matter how he tried, the pail would not turn over to fill up.

I sent someone else who came back screaming that the well was witched. His pail would not turn over to dip up water either. I soon resigned myself to the fact that some people could get water while others could not. I thought it odd that Eric could.

A few people became angry one evening, calling me names and accusing me of being a witch because of the water in the well. I ignored them, letting it all go over my head. They went away. I preferred to think of the water as a gift from the Cosmos.

I certainly was not a witch. Maybe I was simply a water diviner taking after my father.

This is the true story – exactly as it happened.

Desperate for a clear answer, water tests did confirm mold in the barrels.

Beethoven and Sibelius

Ludwig Van Beethoven had become my spiritual teacher through music. As a child, I had struggled to learn to play his compositions on the piano. I would spend leisure time listening to great pianists play his music. One evening a friend brought a record for me to listen to. It was the Emperor Concerto with Artur Rubinstein at the piano.

I lit the fire in the fireplace and lay down on a braided, oval rug to listen. Closing my eyes, I closed out my surroundings and let the music come alive. Rubinstein played with a divine sensitivity of each note – every note perfect in tone. He was at one with his piano.

I allowed myself to open up to the sound. The music entered my body. It played low in my body with low sounds, right down to my feet and would play up my body as the notes went higher. I became the musical instrument with every sound vibrating within me. Up and down, around, down and up, softer and louder, when unexpectedly it aroused my heart region, blossoming into a radiance of the most beautiful feeling I had ever felt. It was all encompassing powerful. To stay with this blissful sensation forever would be all right with me. Basking in it, I could feel the centre radiating outward in beatific love.

For days after that experience, I was gentle and soft. I could call up the feeling easily just by listening to the music. Bliss was mine.

Gradually the experience faded and only the memory was left.

A fascination with Beethoven's mind grew out of that experience. I read everything I could find about the man but could not find the answers I was looking for. Here was a man who obviously wrote music for the spirit, from his own spirit – a man who had great difficulty getting along in this world. He never had the love of a woman in return for his love. Here was a man with a great and wondrous spirit, a man of great depths, ignored by love. Here was a man who was physically deaf and despite his difficult life, wrote the most beautiful music. I was in love with the man who gave me this music.

Having had that experience of opening my heart chakra with Beethoven's music many moons before living at the meditation centre, I was now living with no access to music in my house. I had always had music around me, never knowing life without music, so this was starvation of a different kind.

Our new houseguest, Jackson, a young man running away from college had come to stay with us on the meditation centre. He had arrived very broke as our guests usually did, meaning he could contribute no money toward food. That meant I would have one more mouth to feed, more clothes to wash by hand and more problems to solve for him, which is usually what happened. Not only that, but I would get the flack and blame when people messed up like when, unknown to me, Jackson hung his soaking wet sleeping bag in Bhikhu's cabin. The floor had pools of water on it just before Bhikhu arrived for the night. Bhikhu slipped in the dark. People needed parents and caretakers, and would find them wherever they could. These days it was me. I never knew who would be my next kid.

We had gone to town, shopping for groceries. I had spent every last cent I had on food for the centre with nothing left over. Jackson walked up to the counter and bought a chocolate bar. As I watched in disbelief, he ate every last bite, completely oblivious of me. Constantly, I was in disbelief over the actions of students of meditation. I often wondered why I put up with it all. My children would have loved a chocolate bar. I would have liked an extra quart of milk for them out of this guy's hidden pocket money.

For that, Jackson was sentenced to hard labor. He had come expecting to loaf around and was obviously not used to any hard work. He was sent out to work with Eric, cutting and hauling wood for winter. Expecting him to escape back to the city, it came as a surprise when he blossomed. His weak body became stronger as the days went by. Weeks later, he was still with us, in better health than ever. In all, he stayed three months with us.

Jackson's prized possession was his record player, which he had brought with him along with his clothes. He placed it in the main room.

I could play music at last.

Then one morning, with the older children in school, the younger children playing quietly and the men in the woods, I found myself putting on Beethoven's Emperor Concerto. The record had somehow made its way across the country as my priced possession. Laying the needle on the record, I floated into a chair facing the window with a view of the sky, fields and woods. In total relaxation ... beautiful relaxation, I let myself go. The music and I became one again, in perfect harmony.

In the middle range, the sound entered my heart, blossoming fully as it had done before. The sound went lower and the energy from my heart moved down into the base of my spine. The heat was enormous; filling my lower body with a fire greater than any sexual energy I had ever known. Then it moved slightly forward and up into my belly, heating and blossoming there. As the music came out of the depths and rose, so did the energy. It rose and moved forward into another chakra at my navel, then smoothly back to my heart, blossoming fully in my chest. In my forehead, as though on a television screen, I could see inside my complete chest as clear as if a moving picture had been taken.

A little flame of energy like a fire finger was moving up to my throat and wiggling around in there. It was still in my heart but as though sending a feeler up to see if it could move up. Then it stopped. The finger of fire lowered back to the heart and all eventually cooled down.

Then, I was to experience a throat so sore that I could barely talk. For three days, there was no relief.

This time, I did not wait for Bhikhu to come. I went to find him in the city.

When I arrived, he greeted me cheerfully. We talked some small talk until I, with my hoarse throat, told him about what happened to me. He listened intently but with what I detected as amusement in his eyes.

"Wait here a minute," he said.

As he was walking to the kitchen, he said nonchalantly, as though it was some small matter, "Oh, the Kundalini can't get by your blocked throat chakra because your karma is in there. You have had a habit of building karma with words."

I waited in silence while I figured that one out. Who would know best but the man with whom I often had those noteworthy and unsettling discussions? I was not getting praise for what I had done, just more to think about.

He came back carrying a white cup with purple Violet flowers painted around the sides.

Staring at the cup, I knew he was feeling kindly toward me. We all had learned that whatever the cup looked like that he served to you, it was chosen with a purpose.

Reaching for the cup, I realized it was steaming hot and pulled my hand away.

"Take it," he ordered.

Taking it from him, I realized it was not hot tea. It was steaming hot, thick broth.

"Drink it!" he ordered.

"I can't, it's too hot."

I looked up at him, questioningly.

"Drink it now!" he insisted, looking intently into my eyes.

That hot broth looked like it had more heat than any soup I had ever seen, all stuck in the thickness of a cream colored liquid.

He stood in front of me, towering over me, looking intently at me. So I did, slowly but surely put the cup to my mouth and sipped. It burned my lips and my tongue.

"More!" he commanded.

Another sip and I had burned my mouth and my throat.

Then he relaxed while I was in pain.

I went back to the meditation centre with a burned mouth that lasted three days. Three days in which it hurt to talk and eat.

When it healed, I put my record on again and meditated with it. This time, the Kundalini energy came alive again and moved up into my throat, smoothly flowing through and up into the third eye of my brow, blossoming there, moving up to the top of my head, where I found at least a bud of the thousand petal lotus. I knew my connection with a higher consciousness.

When someone reported to Bhikhu that I must be enlightened because of my chakras opening, I had no knowledge of it until Bhikhu arrived. He asked me to walk with him into the forest.

I had heard that if the lotus blossomed on top of the head, enlightenment was established. Well, I knew what I felt and saw, but I also knew I was not any more enlightened than yesterday or last month. I thought my experiences with energy and explorations in the universe were simply antics like a mischievous child. I likened myself to the one light bulb connected to a larger source of energy that lit up intermittently, but the more I knew, the more I knew I did not know the totality of the cosmos or God. And furthermore, I was not going to pretend any more than that. I was ticked off at whoever reported such a statement, proving I was still very human and not going anywhere.

On the walk in the forest, our discussion turned to music. I favored Beethoven. He favored Jean Sibelius.

"Sibelius is calmer," he told me. "It's like these woods. You know, Sibelius was a hermit much of the time, hiding away by the sea to write. His music reflects his calm nature. Listen to it. You are like Beethoven, lots of ups and downs. You do not stay in the middle. A little more balance is needed. Not much swinging."

"You mean, flatten my emotions?"

"Yes, I mean not so up and not so down."

"But I like experiencing all the emotions. That's life."

We stood there facing each other. I always managed to get into an argument with this man, it seemed.

"Life. You don't know life yet. You are too busy enjoying life here to get on with it. Don't spend so much time enjoying this earth."

He had emphasized 'enjoying this earth'.

"But I like this earth. I love these trees. I don't want to be anywhere else. Furthermore, I'm very attached to it all here. I get high on the colors of nature. And I never get so low as to be depressed. My swings are in the upper range."

"You are in love with Maya … illusions."

Bhikhu turned to walk toward the house, expecting me to follow.

I felt exasperated with him. Always, he threatened my existence. I felt threatened that the relationship I had with my family, with the very earth would be taken away from me. All the talk about life after death and a better life on other planes was a pain to me, especially out here in the forest where I could really enjoy nature.

I stubbornly stood my ground. "I like it here!" I yelled after him.

He did not turn around.

No more was said about that, but on Bhikhu's next trip from the city on the weekend, he brought some records – Sibelius for me and Peter and the Wolf by Sergei Prokofiev for the children.

"A little humor for the children," he said as he handed us the records.

Over the next week, Sibelius and I made our acquaintance. It was certainly picturesque music of nature's wild seas to serene woods. The music was alive and not emotionally flat to my ears.

winter scriptures

To find some privacy, Bhikhu and I strolled in the woods for another talk. For Christmas, someone had given him a pair of leather boots made by Inuit people. His feet were slipping out of control in the snow with no traction under his soles. I gave him my arm to lean on. I wanted him to be above being human, but here I was, holding this giant man up.

"I have no time to meditate. I get no help from Eric in anything. All he can think about is being out in the woods getting firewood. Then he comes back to the house and is a guru for the rest of the evening. The children are not getting any attention from him."

I looked at my teacher to be sure he was listening carefully. He was.

I went on. "When you give discourses, I am always in the kitchen preparing food or getting tea. I miss everything. People sit around discussing the scriptures and I have no time. I feel like I am being robbed of my intelligence. They all know more than I do."

My voice was bouncing off the trees and back in my ears. I did not like my sound.

He said, "There is no food value in feeding intellect with scriptures. You could spend your life studying scriptures and miss what you are meant to learn. You are doing what you need to do."

Unconvinced, I went on, "As an example: Those women – you know who I mean – stayed here all week. With Christmas over, they came here for a holiday. They are housewives who have families. They are perfectly capable women. I worked my butt off for them all week while they meditated. Yesterday, I decided to have some time to myself. I played in the snow with my children. Then, I went to the other cabin to meditate for an hour. When I got back to the house, one of those women was on her high horse because she had not had her afternoon tea served to her by me. She told me I had to make it. I told her to make it herself – that I had just been meditating and she did not have to wait for me. She actually told me I have no right to meditate, that I am here to serve her. That makes me darn mad!"

"Self-destruction in the face of difficulties would be an error, would it not?"

"What do you mean?"

"Listen to yourself. Where is your balance? Why let those poor women destroy you? You are above that. You are capable of more. Do you think if someone told me that I have no right to meditate that I would take him seriously? Why would you?"

He sure could get to me. I nodded. How right! Slippery boots and all, he always had the right answer for me.

eggs and onions

Arranging the menus with inadequate contributions from the many arrivals was constant. Often I confronted my teacher with my problems. He believed we could only accept donations and no one could be turned away. Whose shoulders did that fall on? Mine! And only mine! No one else had to deal with it! Even my husband did not have to deal with it as he went about his outdoor activities.

All night I had tossed and turned. Guests had arrived late last night – at least ten of them and there was no food in the house. I had no money to prepare for guests. I lost sleep wondering how they would be fed in the morning.

No matter what my shortcomings may have been, I always kept up a good front and served good meals but at this breakfast, everyone would know there was no food.

In the morning, I washed and dressed carefully, as usual, but slower. Then, I lit the fire in the wood stove and put the kettle of water on.

People were drifting around. I stood facing the stove, not knowing quite what to do. We had no oats, no bread, and no flour to bake bread as I did every day, or at least I made biscuits if in a hurry. I could not think of anything to feed these people, or my children.

Bhikhu approached and stood by my side at the stove. Knowing something was unusually wrong with me, he asked quietly what was bothering me.

I had complained to him many times before but this time he understood that my present dilemma was more serious to me than usual. I knew that by the quiet gentleness in which he spoke that he understood.

"What have we got?" he asked.

I shuffled around in the cupboard and brought out four eggs and two onions.

"That's it! That's all." I shrugged.

"Good," he answered.

"Good?" I was surprised by his answer.

"Good. Take those two onions; cut them up into small pieces. Scramble the eggs over them. Cook them," he ordered quietly.

Together we huddled over the stove as we cooked the eggs and onions.

"Set the table," he commanded.

I did so, feeling foolish. There were newly arrived quests plus my family and permanent guests – around twenty people for breakfast.

Breakfast was always a happy time for guests from the city. Delight at waking up in the country was always written over their faces. They would arrive at breakfast glowing and hungry.

Everyone sat around the table expectantly. Bhikhu took a place near the stove and I sat across from him. He started the eggs and onions around the table. Each person took a helping and passed the serving plate on. I held my breath for the first people, expecting them to empty the dish, leaving an empty platter for the rest. But it kept going. Each person took a helping and passed it on. Amazed, I could not believe my eyes.

Bhikhu was waiting with me for the platter to return to our end of the table. It passed by my children who helped each other and each had a good portion.

When the platter returned to us, Bhikhu served me, then himself. I looked carefully at all the dishes with breakfast on them and all the people who were talking to each other as usual, as though nothing out of the ordinary had happened.

I was the only one who knew what had just happened. I was the only one who saw.

Bhikhu looked at me intently. I smiled in amazement. "The fish and loaves," I whispered.

"You see, you do not need to meditate as much as the others. Your service does you more good. Life is full of miracles."

I had always known a security that did not come from material wealth. This experience solidified knowing a richer source of wellbeing.

I was to learn another lesson though ...

cheese please

One winter evening after a weekend of feeding a crowd of city people, my cupboard was bare again. Only a small block of cheese was left over. I had children to feed and they had to have a school lunch for the next day.

"Save the cheese for the children." That thought kept repeating in my head. Finally, I hid the piece of cheese in the back of the cupboard behind the pots and pans. No one would find it there, not even a mouse because the cupboard was tin lined. I would give it to my children tomorrow for school lunch. It would not be much but better than nothing.

"God will provide" was a motto that seemed to be repeating in my head a lot with little rhyme or reason. Students liked to believe that they were chosen ones and God would provide.

Two hours after I had carefully hidden the cheese and I was finished cleaning the kitchen for the night, there was a surprising knock at the door. The two male students who traveled with Bhikhu and always came only when he came, walked in. They had not come this weekend. Now they arrived in this late Sunday evening. Accepting of the unusual, as usual, I did not question their arrival. I simply put the kettle on for tea, looking forward to the company. The young man, who was the closest student to Bhikhu, bounced across the room, asking, "Hey, I'm hungry. Have you any cheese?"

A picture of the cheese I had so carefully hidden popped into my head.

"Save it for the children." Those words had run though my head for hours and now they were loud and clear.

The young man smiled expectantly.

Testing! Am I being tested? Thoughts of Bhikhu testing me ran through my head. How did this man know to ask for the very thing I hid? Not only that, but it would have taken these men just the amount of time to drive from the city to arrive at the meditation centre, if they left the city at the time I hid the cheese. It was all very strange.

I was thinking that I must say no – keep it for the children. But I could not be dishonest. I had to give what was asked of me. God had sent this guy for cheese and God would provide for my children.

Sheepishly, I reached into the cupboard and brought out the cheese, which was devoured by the night visitors. When their tea and cheese was finished, they said their thanks and left as strangely as they had arrived.

I stood there looking at the closed door, listening to the motor of their car disappear down the dirt road. It appeared they were traveling hours just to eat a cheese hidden from view. They had asked for and eaten food that was meant for children.

The questions were bountiful. Why had they arrived under the strange circumstances? It was extremely odd. I wondered about what universal energy had provoked their visit to demand cheese. What had I done? What was my role in this matter? I had hoped God would provide and now my children were about to starve. I was to blame. I had given away their food to men who clearly were not starving. I had always thought of my children as my gift in life – my gift from God or the Creator. With such a gift, I had been given the responsibility to look after them. Why had I not protected my children?

God did not provide that night. God did not make up for my poor judgment.

The next day, I had nothing to pack for my children's lunch to take to school and they had minimal breakfast. My children went hungry that day except for my last two dimes that I gave them to go to the store near the school and buy a donut. I was to blame for my children's hunger.

A lesson was obvious. My children were my responsibility. They were dependant on me. No one else would provide if I did not. No one else would feed them. I was to look after my own children first, just as Bhikhu had warned me to do. Then, only then, was I to look after the world, not the other way around.

Teacher's Whiskey

It happened one mid-winter night when there was a big snowstorm.

Bhikhu was teaching in Scotland.

Snow was piled high around our countryside. We were feeling cozy and warm in the log cabin and settled in for a couple of days of not expecting guests. The children were sleeping in the upstairs bedrooms for the night. My husband, his helper Jackson, and I were having tea around the kitchen table when there was a surprise knock on the door.

A snow covered man stood there, saying, "I'm stuck on the road. I'm trying to get to my cabin by the lake."

We invited him in to get warm and dry. Somehow during the evening, just for a bit of entertainment, I brought out the cards. I had not done that on the meditation centre before that night. He was looking for insight into certain problems so I gave a reading of his cards even though I had no idea what information he was looking for.

He seemed happy when I finished, but did not give me any clues that he got an answer.

A couple of hours later, the snow stopped and the guys went out to dig his car out. Once freed, the man decided to continue on to his cabin. We never expected to hear from him again.

After breakfast the next morning, I was angry at both Eric and Jackson. It was unusual for me to say much, but I had enough of what I thought was their lack of caring about my household needs and still acting like they were superior. I gave them a dressing down in strong words.

The sun had been out for hours by noon when there was another knock on the door. The same man stood there with a big smile. He held a large bottle in his hand. He came in, bypassing the guys, and handed the bottle to me. He thanked me for the wonderful reading that answered his problems.

Then, the happy man disappeared as quickly as he came.

I was standing by my stove when he handed the bottle to me and there I stood after he was gone, looking at his gift in amazement. The label said it was TEACHER'S WHISKEY made in SCOTLAND.

The guys were looking and roaring with laughter. They were having a giant joke because they knew something I did not know.

I had never tasted Teacher's Whiskey. The guys insisted I have some. My husband poured it for me straight from the bottle. They watched knowingly.

I put the cup to my mouth. The whiskey ran across my tongue. It was extremely bitter to my taste. I cringed.

They laughed and told me it was payback for my bitter words of that morning.

I did not know what happened to the remainder of the whiskey. It just disappeared.

I was never to know what the man was so grateful for.

I was left with many questions. What unseen power made a stranger go to the store and buy this gift? How on earth was it that this man was the bearer of such a gift to me of Teacher's Whiskey made in Scotland while my teacher was in Scotland? I felt that I was being given a reminder from a long way across the ocean – that distance and separation has no bearing in a connection that overcomes distance and time. And somehow there is a knowing across all space and time.

bigger

A small group of men were staying with us now, helping Eric. It was late in the evening. The children had just fallen asleep. I came down the stairs to find everyone seated around the warm living room fire in the freestanding stove. I took a chair, feeling relaxed and cozy.

As usual, Eric was talking Zen philosophy, rubbing his chin and waving his fingers in the air. He always managed to captivate his audience.

Closing my eyes, I relaxed into meditation. I experienced the usual pleasant feelings. Then suddenly, it was as though I was falling backward. I felt that I must maintain control because falling back seemed to be a black void of unconsciousness. I must stay upright and conscious. Struggling, I opened my eyes. I was getting larger and larger. I was immense. I was a giant. I was sitting in my chair, perfectly straight, perfectly conscious. I knew my body was the same size as all the other little people in the room but *I* was definitely bigger – much bigger than all of them.

Power. I had immense power. I could feel it building. Time stood still. I had found the timeless zone. I could see the people and the world around me were all in 'Time' but 'I' was in a timeless place. I waved my hand in front of me and knew it to be in all positions at all times. There was all time and no time. Everything happened at once and no time. At last, I understood.

Eric had a big ego. I had a fleeting thought about how little he was.

He grabbed his head and cried, "Don't think of me!"

I was amazed. How had he known?

His hand held his head as he cried out again, "Don't! It hurts my head."

I ran out of the room and stood in the far corner of the kitchen.

I could see him even though there was a wall between us.

"Don't think of me," he called desperately.

Deliberately changing my thoughts, he quieted down.

I wondered what he was thinking. Just as I thought about him again, he hollered, "No! Leave my head alone. Don't think of me."

It really was true. He knew when I was thinking of him. I was so powerful that his head hurt. Unbelievable.

Realizing that Bob and Jackson were also scared now, I deliberately worked at coming out of that state. Soon, I was small again, but with the knowledge of my greater self that would always be with me.

Eric would not forget. After years of making me feel small so that he could feel large, he was unforgiving.

The next morning after breakfast, I walked into the living room to find Eric and Jackson just sitting in chairs watching me expectantly as I entered the room. I immediately saw that a clay sculpture I had made just days before and placed it in the middle of the coffee table, was now smashed. I knew Eric had done it. I did not give him the satisfaction of acknowledging my broken artwork.

dark night of the soul

"You are experiencing the dark night of the soul"

My heart ached. I had come to Bhikhu for help. His words were not consoling. The only light in the room came over his shoulder from the window. His face was cast in shadow. Dark sympathetic eyes looked into mine.

We were close. All the months of disagreements and rebellion on my part had not come between us.

Pulling my eyes away, I stared down at the Tarot cards he had dropped on the floor at my feet.

The nine of swords and ten of swords lay there – dark and desolate – suffering pain. How closely they matched my feelings.

"Ah, but don't let that be all. There is also end to delusion. You cannot stay there. You must experience darkness to know light. The dark night of the soul does not last forever."

"Will Eric come back to me?"

"I do not know. Your life does not depend on Eric."

"But the children."

"Your children's lives do not depend on him."

"He should not be allowed to run off and be irresponsible. What sort of teaching is this?"

"It would do you no good for me to order him returned."

"But I'm pregnant!"

"Then you have much to live for."

I stared at him. How could I make him see? How could he understand my pregnant needs? At that moment, I thought this man giving me advice should be reborn as a woman, so that he would understand.

"I love him." I was lying and I knew it.

I was hurt that he was breaking a family connection. I had been another of his conquests but for some strange reason he got stuck to me like glue.

"Love! You call that love! Possessive attachment! You love your children in the most selfless love you know. Love is not selfish, not rooted in your own desires."

"And Eric, does he know love?"

"Eric!" He shook his head. "Eric will keep you from knowing love. Eric will tie up your energy. He will use you. Go! You only think you are unhappy. This is your illusion and delusion. You may not believe me, but there is someone else for you in the future. You will continue to live for many years in a balanced way. It is not time for you to become a renunciant. You must experience earthly life in abundance but with a greater understanding than the average person."

Feeling despondent, I left the room. What I had just heard was not what I wanted to hear. What now?

Eric had left, just walked out. He had gone to the city and not returned. Days went by and eventually the realization hit me that he was gone for good.

I had cut his hair that morning and he dressed in his good clothes for the trip. He had a small overnight bag in his hand as he stood in the doorway before leaving. It was his red plaid jacket in the open doorway that twigged a kind of knowing. I had seen this scene before somewhere, somehow even though it was happening only now. He was promising to just look for work in the city and that he was not leaving for good. Suddenly, I had a gut realization. I knew now what had been bothering me that first day on the meditation centre. That horrible, foreboding feeling was a glimpse at what was happening now. I would lose Eric here. I knew he would leave and not return. But more than that, he would leave when I was feeling most vulnerable.

Then one evening soon after my husband left, I had been sitting by the fire with the monk who stayed on the meditation centre to help me cope with being alone without modern conveniences in the country and the middle of a freezing winter. Being pregnant, falling asleep came easily. I relaxed by the warmth and while we were talking, I fell asleep in my chair.

I woke up with a start. I had been in a room with Eric while he was having sex with another woman. It was so real that I knew for sure it was happening right then and somehow I was a witness.

The monk was still in his chair, watching over me. The Bhikhu was the only person on earth I ever shared my troubles with, so I kept my disturbance to myself that evening.

The following day, I went to the city to find Eric and did. It had been many months since I had been to a restaurant. Being in the city, Eric asked me out to dinner. Even though we had been vegetarians for two years, he wanted steak. As the hunk of red meat was set in front me, he assured me that he was leaving and yes, he had sex with another woman last night – a friend of mine.

He continued talking. "But she was just like an old shoe. Fit well but not exciting."

Eric always had a way of saying hurtful things.

"Why? Why if like an old shoe, why at all?" I was bewildered.

"Some things are necessary. They are out of my control."

His arrogance and lack of sensitivity always got to me.

"I'm pregnant," I said.

"But you were not pregnant when I left."

"You've only been gone a few days. Of course, I was pregnant."

"It must be someone else's." He looked me straight in the eyes as though commanding it to be someone else's.

"You know I've only been with you. You know I never slept around."

"That's been your problem. You are behind everyone else spiritually because you haven't been sleeping around."

"You really believe that?" Those were the most incredible words I ever heard.

"I'm serious. Grow up. Sleep around a little."

"But what about the children, the coming baby?"

"Get an abortion. It's not mine."

My appetite was gone. The food on the table made me feel sick. The poor cow died just to be thrown in the garbage.

Eric was upset that I should ruin his dinner. How could I ever have seen anything worthwhile in this man? I also had been a conquered item in the beginning, but regardless of my initial intuitive dislike of him, I had ignored my strong intuition. I had only myself to blame.

Now I would have to tell my children.

I delayed. Days went by and I did not have the heart to tell them.

"What if dad never comes home?" The children were in their beds. I wished they would sleep, but they were questioning each other on possibilities. I could have gone in then and talked to them but I could not. Because I was pregnant, I had an attachment that I would not have had if I had not become pregnant. I prayed for help and guidance instead.

I had a dream some weeks later. In the dream, my children and I were in a van driving the country road alongside the meditation centre acreage. The road suddenly had a large crevice across it that looked like an earthquake had hit it and we were unable to go any farther. When I woke up, I knew the dream meant our time at the centre was finished. We must move.

We went back to the city.

During my pregnancy, Eric flaunted women in front of me. It was the last straw when he brought a sixteen-year old girl to a party that he also invited me to. I had a long time to remember Bhikhu's advice before it made sense to me and I no longer wanted Eric back.

I had to get even farther away from Eric. He was not physically harming me, but the head games definitely were. I had to stop his head games and the emotional turmoil that he continued to put the children and me through.

starting over again

At six and a half months pregnant, I sold my negative retouching machine for just enough money to board a train with my children and hopefully a month's rent and a little food.

Leaving all our belongings behind for a second time, except for clothing and some bedding, four children and I headed across the country to ... what?

I did not know what we would really find, except it was four days to the farthest place at the end of the earth. I needed to take control of my life and leave Eric behind. I needed to give my children a life other than watching me being a doormat. It had to be a place where we could live with nature on very little money. I decided that was by the ocean and hopefully we could live close enough to walk to a beach. I was looking to the future with simple hope.

I could have gone home to my parents, but I did not want to feel dependently trapped. I needed my freedom.

Just a couple of days after arriving on the coast, my baby was born two and a half months premature. I would again experience a higher power looking after us. I was told my two and a half pound girl may not live, but when I looked at her through the window with all the tubes and so small I was not allowed to touch her, I could see the powerful energy in her hands. I had faith she would live. I thought it ironic that just to prove who her father was, as a newborn she looked like him.

During the next week, I was hospital bound, not realizing I had patient rights and could leave. I had an experience on the third night that cannot be explained. I was woken up by a doctor telling me that I had a uterine infection and must be treated. Then the treatment never happened and no such doctor existed. I did not have an infection. I wondered if this was because during this pregnancy I thought a lot about my grandmother who died of a hospital staph infection three days after giving birth to her fifth child. I had just given birth to my fifth child. Somehow a recreation of her third day had just happened and then did not happen. It was so real that I can still remember what the doctor looked like. That whole experience would prompt me to do midwifery later.

My troubles were not over yet. It was a time when babies were being snatched from single parents. All because I was separated and admitted that when I entered the hospital, I had been placed in a large ward of unmarried women who were giving birth out of wedlock.

A social worker surprised me by standing over me and looking down at me while I was in my hospital bed right after I gave birth. She told me she wanted my baby, to put her up for adoption for no other reason except that I had no husband and had given birth in an unmarried women's ward at the hospital. She reasoned that I already had four children and did not need a fifth. I told her my baby was not available for adoption. She was relentless, putting on hard pressure every day and continued to bother me over weeks.

Eventually, my baby was five pounds, healthy and due to be released from the hospital. The sergeant-at-arms social worker arrived at my apartment with papers to sign as her final step to stealing my baby. She stood on a step below me on the long, straight staircase as I opened my door. We were now eye to eye even though she was a big woman almost a foot taller than me. I was a mother protecting her babies and I was transforming into thunder and lightening. I felt my energy grow large. I threatened to throw her down the stairs if she did not leave me alone.

Much to my surprise, without another word she turned around. I watched her back as she went quickly down the stairs. I never heard from her again, not even to retaliate my threat.

Would I have carried out the threat? Taking a baby away from an unwilling mother can provoke an unexpected reaction. We see it clearly in animals that go quite crazy with grief when their young are ripped away. We humans are no different; we have basic instincts.

This was not a case of fight or flight. My baby was behind locked doors. Hospitals follow guidelines set out by social workers regarding apprehension of children. I could get behind the locked doors to sit with my baby only in the last couple of weeks, but she was still in a locked cage. There was no way I could gather all my children together and run away. Going the legal route after the fact was no answer. I had seen parents, especially in aboriginal families, lose their children with no help from the legal community that also overwhelmingly supported social workers' opinions. Regardless of my aversion to violence, and regardless of all the teachings, I was going to defend my motherly right to my baby and confront the aggressor right on. Fight or Flight? I had only one choice and I was not about to be passive.

My baby came home with me.

I recovered quickly. I did get on with my life as a single parent and in the process, I found ME again and boundless happiness.

Eric followed quickly. Just weeks after I brought my baby home, he arrived with his girlfriend, someone I had already met. He dumped her on my doorstep for me to take care of, which I did. He took off to India.

How could I look after his girlfriend? I had already healed. I had an open heart and it was like I was still on the meditation centre looking after whoever came my way.

I heard from him again when months later he was stranded in Europe. This man had never once asked about the children nor cared for them with one penny, but he wanted money from me with a promise to come back to me. His girlfriend thought I should send money to him. I needed to tell her that I had children to look after and I was finished with him. I emphasized that I did not care if he ever found his way back to his country.

Months later, he made another conciliation attempt by sending a gift via a monk accompanying Bhikhu on a visit with me in my home. The monk handed me a star ruby of considerably large size. I sent it back.

My gift in life was that my children and I were in the care of a higher power.

What could I say in the end about the relationship Eric and I had? Maybe we were time-limited explorers and my time with him just ran out.

together

Missing from this picture are the little dog, a rabbit and a duck that lived with us now. Still a single parent, I wanted to give my children what I thought would make their lives more fulfilled in starting over. I taught my sons oil painting. I had my guitar and gave another one to my second son. My oldest son passionately built a science lab in a closet; he found the lab supply outlet and became a youngest regular customer. My oldest daughter was in ballet lessons. Our entertainment on a tiny budget was to go as a family to the library or to explore Chinatown, and we had the beach a short walking distance from our house. We had nature in abundance just as I had hoped for. Life was good.

looking back

Had I learned my lessons? I still had a way to go.

I faced many hurdles in resettling. I had promised my children a trip to the beach as soon as we found an apartment. After spending two nights in a hotel, and many phone calls to find housing, it was clear that no one wanted us because we were a family with children. Help from all services including social services and the YWCA was refused because I admitted to having a month's rent money.

On day three, one phone call found a true guardian angel. It turned out the man had a habit of housing women needing help in houses he managed.

The children and I had walked the city. On the way to see him, mid-span of a major bridge after walking the bridge a couple of times because we were lost, I felt something odd, like something snapping open.

When we finally arrived at his door, the man took us under his wing. He piled us into his car, picked up our belongings from the train station and then put us in an unfurnished apartment. He did all that without a hint of expecting anything in return except the rent money.

That night, we rolled out our blankets and pillows onto the floor. Lying on the hard floor all night, I thought I was in false labor so I kept my promise to my children the next morning. At a store a couple of blocks from the house, I bought some picnic food and then we went by bus to the beach.

As the sun was setting at nine in the evening, I could no longer deny that I was in excruciating, hard labor. I needed to take my children home on a bus across town, not knowing how to care for them and go to the hospital. While in labor and scared that I might deliver a premature baby on the bus, I imagined needing social services to help and knew that was an extremely dangerous route. I did not know what else to do.

When we walked through the front door of our new home, a couple living in the main floor apartment met us and introduced themselves. She was also pregnant and he worked as a longshoreman. Immediately, they offered to look after the children so that I could go to the hospital and not worry about them.

For a second time in two days, we were being looked after and danger was averted. Facing life and death with my baby and knowing life would win was a third in three days.

After a week in the hospital, I walked home to find my children had been well taken care of, but they were suffering emotionally because I had disappeared in a strange city. It was a tough half hour trying to get my bearings in an unfurnished apartment and make the world right with my children. After a half hour of feeling quite devastated about what I had done to my children, and wondering how to survive going forward, I was standing by the window and looking across the city to the mountains when I heard the words clearly in my head, "You can have it any way you want." I realized it meant that I could sink or swim. In that moment, I chose swim and recovered immediately.

I needed to walk to and from the hospital to visit my baby because I had no money for bus fare. But through it all, I was physically and emotionally strong and my children were just fine after all, now that I was home with them. My aura tended to expand outward very large and I had to work at keeping myself in control. It was a happy aura and I could feel it was bright and beautiful.

I was so extremely happy and optimistic that I brought with me my old habit of wanting to share my good fortune with everyone. I wanted to help others the way I had been helped.

Within a few months, I managed to find a house by the beach just as I had hoped so that my children and I had easy access to fresh sea breezes, sand and the ocean. I would lie in the sand and really study the grains of sand that in the sunshine were filled with color and light. I felt looked after by a higher power.

I again became a magnet. The house was constantly filled with guests from near and far. I continued to believe that God would provide so long as I was looking after everyone. I was still sharing what little my children and I did have. All my life, I had no interest in amassing material things or money; those things would easily slip through my hands and be gone, but my children and I were losing faster than I could keep up.

As it happened, one day when my house was especially crowded and, in an unusual move, I had even given my bedroom away so that I literally had nowhere to sleep but perhaps the floor somewhere or the bathroom, and I certainly did not have enough money to feed the group, Bhikhu arrived with no forewarning. He asked to see my friends.

He sat on the only chair in the living room and looked impressive in his robes. My friends assembled on the cushions around the rug. I stood in the doorway to the kitchen. Everyone was silent. I watched as Bhikhu's eyes scanned each person and then looked even deeper. I knew him well enough by then to know that something did not please him.

Instead of a group discussion that I expected, he decided to meet each person individually. As each person left the room, they did not speak to me as they left the house.

After the last person, he stood up and towered over me. He said, "You must use discrimination. There is a difference between helping the needy and helping people to be selfish and lazy."

Eric's girlfriend hung on tight and continued a certain habit. Whenever she saw me looking nice in something, I could see the tentacles in her eyes. My clothing would disappear. She gave birth to a baby boy by a new boyfriend, then her parents came from another province and took her home.

Bhikhu made several visits to me in my new life a long way from the meditation centre. Then, without asking my permission, he dropped a couple of novice monks into my home and he left the city. A new man in my life was not tolerant of them being looked after by me while they displaced my son from his bedroom and they sat around every day. The tables were turned; after a couple of weeks he got rid of the monks. That was the last time Buddhist monks came to my home.

After many years of going our separate ways, memories of Bhikhu stir up a lot of fondness. Looking back, we had a few skirmishes and I find a lot of humor in our relationship, especially in our skirmishes. I would not change my experience of knowing him.

Was he the golden eagle of my dream? Probably.

☆
◯

Just another Story

I DID IT

She, a perfectly developed baby, would have to fight her way out of the womb and into the world. The day she was born changed her life.

The question is: What is an accident? What does the alignment of the stars have to do with making things happen and making people act the way they do, resulting in a particular outcome for a life? Was her destiny predestined? Where were her guardian angels? Was she supposed to learn something in this school of material, physical life on earth? What was it?

It happened in the middle of a warm June night in a major city hospital. It was the early 1960's and that hospital had a reputation for not allowing people to enter at night. One woman had taken a taxi to the same hospital in late evening and was met at the locked door by a nun dressed in black trimmed in white. The nun had answered the buzzer, but in no uncertain terms, sent the pregnant woman in labor away. The taxi driver had waited, knowing what to expect. He drove the woman to another hospital at no charge.

This night, a pregnant woman did get into the hospital just before the doors were locked. In the middle of the night after a few hours of labor, a doctor was called to attend the premature birth. He refused to get out of bed, telling the nurse he would attend in the morning. Instead of calling for other help, the nurse thought she could stop the birth from happening until the doctor would arrive in the morning.

The nurse used hard hands and arm muscles to hold the baby back. Eventually, the baby slid out regardless of the pressure. She was badly bruised and looked like she had been injured in a war. She had suffered oxygen deprivation as her cord had already quit transferring oxygen from the placenta.

The baby spent time in the nursery, kept away from the prying eyes of parents with the excuse that her birth was premature. The mother was not allowed to hold her baby and certainly not allowed to feed her. Instead, nurses pumped her with bottles. While one nurse was feeding the baby from a bottle and having a conversation with another nurse, she was not watching as the baby stopped swallowing and more importantly, she had stopped breathing. The baby's lungs were filling with fluid. In other words, the nurse was drowning the baby. It was minutes that the baby had no oxygen for a second time.

The parents may never have found out what happened to their baby, but by chance, a nurse on the ward had gone to high school with the father of the baby. She stopped him in the hallway to tell him the story of what happened.

Brain damage was not evident until the baby girl was a few months old. When she did not develop normally and do what other babies her age were doing, she was diagnosed with Cerebral Palsy.

Her prognosis was a shortened life and certainly that she would never be able to do what normal people dream of doing, like marrying and having children.

As she grew, there were many attempts to change the course of her brain damage and repair it. There was Patterning which was people working together to move her body through the patterns of normal development, starting with crawling. There were several recommended operations to supposedly lengthen her ankle and leg muscles that were spastic. Through it all, the child kept smiling and laughing over private tears and fears.

Her father put together a tandem bicycle so that they could whiz around the streets and exercise her at the same time. He gave her happy sunshine that he hoped would balance her life.

Regardless, as she grew, it became more and more difficult to use a walker. The hope that she would eventually be able to walk on her own finally gave way to a necessary wheelchair.

For her, it was like fighting her way out of a paper bag. She had dreams and wishes, but her body was a handicap.

She did marry. In her wedding vow she said, "I take this awful man to be my wedded husband." She meant to say "lawful". He was somewhat challenged and in his frustration, he beat her regularly. Her wedding vow was somehow not a mistake.

She divorced him. One dream had been achieved and dispelled.

Thieves often surround people who cannot defend themselves. She was gang raped by someone she thought was a friend who brought his friends. She became pregnant.

No amount of persuasion would convince her to have an abortion. She wanted her baby. She would have someone to love and care for.

With support by caring people, she gave birth to a healthy baby and cared for him mostly by herself.

It was not long before she became pregnant a second time. She had thought he was safe because she met him in church. He stole her wheelchair.

This time, a nurse at the hospital started a case to have the baby taken from her. In order to prove her case, she overdosed her patient with painkiller drugs to the point where the patient could barely function even to care for herself.

People came out of the woodwork to defend the young mother. She took her baby home.

Over the years, there were many fights. There were always people who were critical of her disability and thought she should not be a mother with children. She fought back. She took parenting courses, one after another. She tried to follow all social services advice and rules.

One fight after another meant that her life was one of fear from one day to the next. Mostly, she never knew who was her true friend and who was knifing her in the back. There were times when she would close her blinds because social workers had been peeping in her windows and drawing wrong conclusions. There were times when she wailed, cried and threatened when people made accusations and felt they had a right to examine every inch of her life. Living in a fishbowl could best describe her situation. At times, she refused to have housekeeping help in order to protect her family from too much criticism and to have a bit of privacy that normally people take for granted. But, she was determined and fought on.

Her goal was to be a responsible parent until her youngest child was an adult. Through all the years, her determination never wavered.

I asked her where she got her strength from, especially because it needed to be sustained over so many years.

She said, "My grandmother! She appears to me all the time. My dad's mother is my guardian angel."

Her grandmother had been her protector in life but died just before her first pregnancy.

Then came the day when she entered a care home where she would have some assistance. She had always prided herself on independence. She did not want to be there but her sons were ready and assisted in the move. She was now in her fifties with grey hair; she had outlived her prognosis and she had lived her dreams. Always finding joy in life, she was surprised to be enjoying her new life and new friends.

Her sons, who were now adults had just been visiting her and were walking away down the hallway. Her father stood by her side, watching her watching her sons.

Turning toward her father, she smiled, "I did it, Dad. I did it!"

Just another Story

WHO ARE THESE CHILDREN

where are my beads

Why do we have awakening memories very suddenly like a lightening strike? Where do they come from? Awakening memories happen to children, sometimes sustained in daily life and sometime very fleetingly. Little children will often tell us stories about the circle of life.

As a small child, she would often and for years, wake out a night's sleep and her first thoughts were that she wanted her beads. She needed them to do beading. Her tiny, colorful beads were somewhere in a small wooden box with tiny drawers. From her bed, her eyes would scan the room. She was looking for her beads that were no longer there, and what about these floors? The floors were supposed to be ground, not wood.

She had no concept of reincarnation in those young years. She only knew that she was in a different environment than where she had been living. As she grew, there were questions about heaven and earth as described by the church, but the questions did not touch on knowing her inner self. There was no connection that she could make. Her knowing was waking up wanting beads that belonged to her and that she preferred everything about the outdoors. She wanted to run barefoot and free.

As an adult, the memory of wanting her beads is still vivid. She always keeps vials of colorful seed beads around for comfort.

She would look across the vast prairies and feel what had gone on before, because history lives forever in the fiber of the open air.

This story is mine.

Beading came naturally to me. I spent a whole summer teaching my daughters how to do beading. Throughout the summer, it was as though I was teaching girls who were the age I lost my beads.

circle of life

My granddaughter was three when she told a story as she was drawing at my kitchen table.

She said, "Gramma, this message is for you from your mother."

(I just happened to be testing a new camera that very hour and caught her in a photo as her story unfolded.)

She then described the picture, in which I am standing by a body of water, crying with big tears running down my face. A reflection of my face is seen in the water. My mother is in the air overhead.

My granddaughter said the letters surrounding my mother is a message from my mother telling me not to cry or be sad because she is ALIVE and I should look at my reflection in the water as a peaceful mirror image of life.

This was quite an elaborate story coming out of a girl who just turned three. She had never seen me cry or heard of my grief. I was not a person who would ever cry in front of anyone about anything. I never talked about my sadness over my mother's death to anyone. This tiny girl was getting her information from some unseen source and certainly beyond the knowledge base of a three-year old child.

She then continued drawing as though nothing out of the ordinary had occurred.

Then, unprompted and all the while continuing to draw, she matter-of-factly told a story of grandmothers being born as babies, then becoming a mother, then being a grandmother, then dying and being born again.

What was even more extraordinary was that my mother had died just prior to this little girl's conception. She had never met her great-grandmother and had never seen a picture of her. However, she had been to visit her great-grandfather just months before she drew this picture. She woke up in the morning in the house her great-grandmother had lived and described a visitation by her great-grandmother during the night. A photo album was brought out. Out of many pictures of various people, she pointed to a picture of her great-grandmother as she had seen her and spoken to her during the night.

who is this child

From his birth, he was already grown up and had a difficult time being a baby.

He was still a tiny baby when I first read a story to him. His eyes read me as a person as I was reading the book.

He had only turned one when his cousin was born. After a visit, he was dressed in his coat when it was time for him to leave. The baby was across the room in an infant chair on the floor. Without a word, he walked over to her, leaned over and put his hand on her forehead. After a long pause with his hand on her forehead, he then walked away deep in thought and again without a word, he left the house with his mother.

What I witnessed was a small boy who had the stature of a man, walk with a purpose to lean over the child and bless her. I saw that this boy had been either a priest or a doctor and had been doing this motion many times before.

Then his brother was born. He has been extremely happy and acts like his brother's caretaker rather than merely a brother. At three years old, he is trying to parent his mother. He tells her how to do things. He edits her language. He tells his mother stories about how he parented his children when he was a father of two daughters. He is certain he wants to be a father again.

This three-year old boy is already well known for his care of other children and for his kindness to all animals. He has recently been given an award for being a best friend in daycare. When asked why? He explained that he helped a girl who fell and hurt herself.

brothers

It started out to be a good day in the summer of 1988. He was in the pasture, tending to his horses. The warmth of sunshine on his face, and the gentle breeze felt good. Buttercups in abundance were beneath his feet. He hopped onto his horse, a golden mixed breed of no special standing in the midst of pure bred horses in the pasture, but to him, this horse with a heart of gold was his favorite. They rode bareback together for a while and then headed back to the barn. At the barn door, he let his horse run back to the pasture.

The radio kept him company while he was sorting tools in the barn. The news came on. In the middle of the news about the Olympic games held in Seoul, South Korea, Korean music played in the background.

The music was having a strange effect on him. Then, Korean music was transporting him into knowing himself as an American soldier in Korea and into the horror of war. He became overwhelmed with awakening memories of a previous lifetime.

He was experiencing all over again being on a train with a group of American soldiers. They were supposed to be going home after long combat. Home for him meant going home to Montana where the love of his life, his blond wife was waiting for him.

North Korean soldiers stopped the train. They quickly boarded the train and shot all the American soldiers.

He remembered being shot in the stomach. The pain was excruciating and he was feeling it all over again. It was a bloody wound. He died.

He experienced again that on leaving his body in death, a young man on the other side immediately appeared to help him cross over and helped to calm him in the shock of it all.

He recognized the young man. He is his older brother now in this present life.

As children in this life, his older brother saved him several times from being hurt in accidents. Always a curious kid about machinery, his brother's quick actions saved the four-year old boy's hand from going through a wringer of an old type washing machine. His brother took him down from a tractor he was trying to drive as a five-year old. When he was on fire because of another kid's antics, his brother knew exactly what to do to put the fire out; burns did happen to the boy's face but were minimized by his older brother's quick actions. In this life as children, his brother had been constantly watching over him.

In this life, the older brother had recurring lucid dreams of having been killed by a wolf in a forest. According to his dreams, he would have died prior to the death in the train.

The man who was shot in the stomach had abdominal problems right from birth.

Along with the awakening memories that he experienced in the barn, he now had clear memory of Korean geography that did not come from any previous knowledge in this lifetime. He could name places, rivers, things that one had to be there to know. On checking out maps and history books, his Korean names and knowledge of terrain were completely correct. Even the name of the train and history of what happened on that train was correct.

Needless to say, he does not want to hear Korean music.

As a result, he was now suffering post-traumatic stress disorder. His dilemma was how to explain to a present wife and family that the pain and trauma are from another lifetime and are as real as if it was happening right now? He was not able to hide his suffering of war, a painful death and being forced to leave the love of his life.

A loveless marriage already in big trouble was now heading for disaster. His wife never did honor for better or worse, sickness or health. It was her way or the highway, but his family kept him from simply taking off down the highway in search of another woman and a former lifetime.

All his life, he had a knowing of something sad and a feeling of loss and loneliness, but he never knew what it was about. Now, grief was reawakened. For months, he grieved all over again for the blond woman who had been his wife and for his lost life in Montana. He wanted to be with her no matter what her age or his age, if only he could find her. Then, after his divorce was final, he had a feeling his beloved wife in Montana was no longer there to be found.

He has had an especially lonely life since that awakening memory. For him, a blond woman in Montana was and is his one and only love.

☆ ☆ ○○ ☆

Just another Story

DINNER INVITE

"I'd like you to come to dinner Saturday night." The voice on the other end of the telephone was the Australian professor's wife. They were new to our country when our first visit together had turned into a disaster. My family was renting a cabin on an island for the summer. After getting off the ferry and driving to our cabin, she needed to use a bathroom. We only had an outdoor wooden outhouse that I thought was kind of pretty sitting there in the forest. She freaked out at the thought of using an outhouse. In a panic, she insisted they leave right away and she literally ran to get into their car. They sped off to sail away on the next ferry.

I answered her, "I'd love to come to dinner. See you then. Should I bring something?"

"Just yourself," was her answer.

Saturday night, I arrived at their house, excited to talk with grownups.

I was introduced to a young man who was an English professor at the university. He melted into the background as his wife Opal was introduced. They were a couple from New York. She was introduced as a child psychologist. It was obvious right away that this vivacious blonde had more than her share of self-assurance and had no trouble taking over air space as she moved her face too close to mine in the greetings.

The table setting told me that these people were the only other dinner guests.

Opal started the conversation across the table from me. "You are the one who lived on the island?"

I had visions of our outhouse being discussed.

"Yes."

"Oh, and what are you doing now?"

We had hardly been introduced when I suddenly felt like protecting myself, but I plunged ahead.

"I am going north to spend a few months in an Inuit village.

"Really? You've got children, haven't you?"

"Yes."

Looking around at the food in front of us and wanting to involve others in the conversation, I said, "This food looks good."

The hostess jumped in, "My husband spent all afternoon cooking while I read a book. He loves to cook."

Opal was eyeing me and I could feel it. She let fly, "What could you accomplish by having your kids out of public schools?"

"Many things. Going north is an example. It is first-hand education on Inuit culture. The children will get individual learning depending on their age."

Large plates of food were being handed around so that guests could to take their desired portions.

Opal challenged, "But who needs individuals in our society? We need to fit people into the mainstream better."

"Why?" our host asked.

"For political reasons for one," Opal answered.

I asked, "What do you mean?"

"Well, you have to keep people in tow or they can't look after themselves. They are deprived people if they are not kept in the mainstream. They can't function."

I said, "Some of our better minds have not been to public schools in their younger year. Take Margaret Mead and Albert Einstein."

"Hogwash!" Opal was angry and I wondered where it was all coming from.

I noticed our hostess had disappeared and we had barely begun eating.

I picked at my food for a minute, then laid down my fork and said quietly but forcefully, "I do believe in educating my children as individuals who can and will think for themselves, and who will keep their creative energies alive from childhood to adulthood. I want my children to question everything and decide for themselves what is good."

We argued for several more minutes.

The hostess returned and sat in her place at the table again. She looked confused as she sipped wine. She was obviously not hungry.

Opal's husband, whose name I had already forgotten, asked, "Why are you going north? What do you hope to find?"

I looked around the table and felt like I was in the wrong story. Opal was vividly hostile and everyone else seemed confused. We had all been picking at our food and the host, who had spent his day cooking, was watching in dismay.

"Why would I go north with my family?" I repeated. "It will be the change I'm looking forward to. Can you imagine all that clean air? No pollution! Just think what it would be like – no cars with all their noise and pollution. I'm looking forward to living in a society where honesty is the keyword – where a man's word is binding ..." my voice trailed off as I realized that in this group, it was more bait.

Opal jumped in, "Don't you think you owe it to your children to raise them in the south and send them to proper schools?"

"No, Opal. I think I owe it to my children to let them experience a society not ruined by white men – a place of clean air and free from war."

"What's wrong with war?" Opal asked.

Now I could not believe my ears. I looked at her in disbelief. My voice got more persistent. "What's wrong with war? Just look at your Vietnam War! What's not wrong with it?"

Opal responded in a high pitch. "We educate our soldiers. All they have to do is be drafted for three years to defend their country and then they have their education paid for. They can even go to college. Even poor black men can get their education this way."

"You mean these men have to go to Vietnam and maybe kill someone or be killed, but if they survive that physically and emotionally, they get their education paid for?" I asked.

"Yes."

"And that's alright with you?" I asked.

Opal was yelling now. "What's wrong with killing someone if they get their education out of it?"

I was shocked. All I could see was a wild-eyed monster with blonde hair across the table from me.

I responded, "You! You're a child psychologist and you think like that? You think there is nothing wrong with that?"

I noticed our hostess's chair was empty again.

I continued, "I have heard how these men come back from war so emotionally depressed and broken up. Some are crippled beyond repair with lost limbs and all kinds of injuries, and some never come back to children who need them. You think that's all right? And what on earth are they defending their own country against? They're in Vietnam, not in America."

Opal and I were in a match, hurtling accusations of wrong thinking back and forth.

Escalating, Opal dealt the blow she thought would throw me to the ground; she accused me of polluting her world by having too many children.

At that point, our hostess reappeared and stood near the table. She looked around at all of us. She spoke calmly. "Guess where I've been." She paused and we all waited for the big surprise.

She was now wide-eyed, shaking her head. "I've been reading this book today about the guests who came to dinner and fought with each other. I have been so disbelieving that it could happen to me that I keep going back upstairs to look at the book again. I just can't believe it!"

I was disbelieving, too. How could they have invited this horrible person to dinner? How could they have done this to me? But I assumed it was an accident, that they really did not know her very well. I had to give my friends the benefit of the doubt.

I went to the kitchen to help clean up. Hardly any food had been eaten but dinner was over.

Opal and her husband, who was still nameless and spineless to my mind, left the house in a huff.

I apologized and left, too. I was outraged at the thought of this monster counseling parents and children in our country. And who let her into our country?

I went home and soon got caught up in all the many tasks to arrange our trip north. The memory of that evening still caused knots to form in my stomach. In the end, even though I could never condone Opal and I hated the idea that she was a counselor, it was my own behavior that bothered me. I wondered how I could have changed the evening. I had brought my outhouse to dinner – my foul mouth.

☆ ☪ ☆

Just another Story

A PLANE RIDE TO THE MOON

Bulging Mexican baskets woven with colors of red, pink and green throughout, and ropes tied around to hold them shut were lined up on the airport floor along with the only two tiny suitcases we owned. My children, three girls aged four, five and nine, and two boys aged twelve and fourteen, looked as colorful as the baskets with their beaming faces and colorful jackets. I surveyed our scene and was amused. I felt that everyone who could see us would feel the adventure we were on. We stood out quite well against the grey floor.

My children hugged the counter as the ticket agent issued our seats and checked our colorful luggage. We were on our way to the far north.

The first flight took us across Canada and this, in fact, was our first airplane to anywhere. Then we found our second flight to take us halfway north to a town by the Hudson Bay. There we were to change flights to fly into our destination of a tiny village farther north.

We landed at the midpoint north and outside the plane window we could see Inuit faces. My children were all glued to the windows. We looked in awe. Real Eskimos! Real Eskimo parkas!

We were the last ones out of the plane and stood looking as the Inuit people all disappeared into the village after being there to greet us. I was left with an impression of softness and gentleness.

We enquired about our next flight. We were told that the plane would leave tomorrow as planned.

The high school dormitory had small rooms where travelers stayed. We had two small rooms for the night. My children made friends immediately with the school children who were in their teens. Several students were from the village where we were going. My teenage boys were off to a head start.

The Inuit girls played with my younger children and showed their special love of children. We all ate together in the school cafeteria and I did not have to prepare a thing. I felt a sense of freedom and relaxation I had not felt in a long time. A good beginning, I thought.

I fell asleep with soft Inuit voices floating in my head and the harsher voices of bush pilots sifting through the wall. They were talking about a broken airplane.

In the morning, my children and I lined up around the little World War II airplane with pontoons on and a glass bubble on top.

"Nope. No flight this morning."

"How come?" I asked.

"Broken. Can't fly."

"When?" I asked.

"Maybe this afternoon."

"Okay, we'll be back."

He was not giving out much information, I thought.

"Oh, well, let's explore," I said to my children.

The air was the cleanest I had breathed in years. The water of the bay was clean and clear blue, a jewel of cleanliness that you could see into for many feet below the surface. We were happy, so why get excited about staying longer. This situation went on for three days with no flight information.

"Hey, Mom!" My excited nine-year old daughter came rushing in. "He taped the airplane."

My sons had just come from the airstrip and stood in the doorway with strange looks on their faces.

"Yeah, Mom, the pilot put a band aid on the airplane. I saw him do it. He says we're going north before it freezes up."

"Are you sure?"

"We saw him do it."

This time several voices chimed together, "We have to go now."

I could hardly believe my ears but we grabbed our bags and headed for the airplane. Sure enough, they were loading.

To board the plane we scrambled over our luggage, which became the floor. Ugh! What had I packed that would be broken?

There were four seats and two benches in the back for passengers. We shared the seats with traveling Inuit people.

How this contraption could fly was beyond me. It looked old, rusted and totally decrepit.

We were off!

My seat was wobbling and swinging into the aisle by several inches. My sons sat with white faces and tried to care for their younger sisters.

Below, the world was white with pothole after pothole of blue water. It all looked clean and undisturbed forever into the horizon and in time. It looked quiet and the roar of our airplane motor seemed louder because of the silence below.

Hours later, we started to come down at dusk. The earth came closer.

Then there was a sudden impact as we cracked through a thin layer of ice. Water splashed around the windows in giant waves that seemed to engulf us in the sea. We floated to the surface and motored slowly to the shore.

Shook up, I looked at the children who were looking white faced and jarred.

We had arrived and were taken to our new home by Inuit men who carried our luggage.

On the way to our home, small Inuit children were walking behind us, but they were not simply walking, they were mimicking our white-man walk. We apparently were funny.

We found our home warm and the freezer was full of arctic char, a gift to us by these generous people.

The children would make the most of their relationships with the village people. They would experience the culture by sharing daily life with the children and teenagers. My children would have intimate experiences with all the children in the village who were at home in each other's homes. Most people were related one way or another. In fact, children slept everywhere and no matter the weather, they were running from one house to another without parkas.

The small children would attend the schools. The boys would experience hunting and gathering, food of the north, real igloos on hunting trips, wearing clothing and boots made by Inuit women, affairs of the heart with girls and the insane knife throwing jealousy of an Inuit boy.

Inuit women taught me how to crochet men's hats and to sew parkas of the region designed for maximum protection from the weather. Every piece of clothing was designed with a purpose, and that included the men's hats. Also, the design of clothing marked the region. I also learned how to braid the colorful lanyards used in their parkas. It took a few tries, but then it was so much fun to see the weaving of colors come together.

Going to church meant having to breath the heavy aroma of seal.

We were given a share of food along with everyone else. We had caribou at Christmas. We were given Polar Bear meat along with all the villagers. Polar Bear smelled so strong that even marinating could not help. I could not cook it and gave it back.

I had heard that Inuit people saw things in the round. I understood the round better than linear thinking. I was standing on a round earth floating in a vast universe. Of course, I had always known that and touched on it in the prairie winters when I would lie in the snow and contemplate the universe. But where I now stood, it felt so remote from society and linear thinking that it was as though I was floating in the universe. It was all so close that I could put out my hand and feel the fiber of space. My roots were evident to me the day I went beyond the village to dig through the snow to find a few dried grasses to put into a vase for my table. I knew now for sure that I was a farmer and not a hunter and gatherer.

Time seemed different up here. Clocks seemed almost ridiculous here, where during the winter there was almost no daylight, and looking after the family and needs of the home were of paramount importance. Clock time was an illusion of the white people who came from the south. The visitors expected meetings to happen on the dot by the clock when in fact, a home might need water or a child was in need of care; the Inuit people may arrive very late to a meeting.

This place was so far away, so remote from the south with not even communication by telephone that it was like being on the moon. It was so close to the sky that the vast white earth was lit every night with the most colorful lightshow of the aurora borealis. I would stand in the snow, listening to the concert of music like a full orchestra playing loudly along with the lightshow.

Marc Chagall had always been my favorite painter. I now understood his paintings that had always struck a chord of excitement within me. Chagall painted everything and everybody having no up and no down, just floating around in all sorts of relationships. What a freeing revelation! It made the best sense to me that I now saw my life in the round like a Chagall painting. It was a kind of awakening.

When I saw an Inuit man on the roof of his home one night, just getting a little closer to the sky, I related him back to Chagall and his paintings. That man on the roof was a recognized artist worldwide. He became my best friend. I understood him.

The Inuit artist and I were kindred spirits. It was his idea that we do art together and learn from each other.

I had been in his studio watching him paint. I took a liking to the two large paintings he was working on. I could not afford to buy them so I said nothing of my wish to own the prints. At Christmas, he came running through the snow with two rolls of paper in his hands. He had read my energy and gave me the gift of his prints.

Just another Story

SHOES OR WINGS

A funny thing happened on the way to the – no not the forum. This is MY story. A funny thing happened on the way to my meeting about Lucid Dreaming and Astral Travel. I was attending out of curiosity about what other people were experiencing and how such a meeting would be conducted.

I debated wearing my comfortable running shoes, but decided to dress up a little. I drove across town with expensive shoes on my feet. At my destination, I got out of the car and on stepping onto the pavement, one shoe broke apart and one whole side looked like it sprouted a wing outward. I walked about ten steps and the other shoe did the exact same thing. I suddenly had no walking shoes, just soles with wings like I was to fly. I shuffled to the meeting a block away.

It was a shoeless meeting, so I was glad to discreetly discard my wings inside the entryway and hide them in my backpack.

Every now and then throughout the meeting I would be quite distracted with thoughts of my shoes that I found hilarious. I had a hard time to not burst into laughter.

Meanwhile, everyone was being so serious.

I kept wondering how come my shoes sprouted wings when I was going to a meeting about astral travel, leaving me without walking shoes. I was wondering how I would transport my body back to my car in this cold winter evening.

In the end, I walked back in my socks and simply told my feet not to get cold on the pavement.

I survived another very strange experience.

Life can be funny and fun when you are your own sideshow.

☆ ☆○☆

Just another Story

COINS

What is it about coins? Do coins cause transcendence of logical thinking?

Need and greed for money do cause some human beings to act irrationally. But, there is another story about coins.

I come from a long line of verbal storytellers. In my young years, as I would sit on the floor in the dim light of coal oil lanterns, my father and my uncles would tell stories. I grew up with intriguing stories about money fires. Following their storylines, my visual mind would picture these same men sitting around a fire in the vast prairie at night and when they put the fire out, there would be real money coins that they picked up and held.

I never knew if the stories were true. I only knew that my father did not lie.

When he was a much older man, on one of my visits home, I asked my father about those stories.

He said they were true. He took the opportunity to do his favorite activity; he repeated his stories and I was drawn in completely, all over again.

There are endless stories about people finding coins in odd places; these coins have often been associated with angels or spirits of loved ones leaving signs of existence and ongoing caring. Until a person experiences finding these coins for themselves, there is often the question of whether or not they are just finding lost coins and that is that.

Then it happened to me. Someone close to me, died. Coins started appearing everywhere I was. If I walked in the forest, I would find coins on my path where few people walked, not once but so often that I had to take notice. If I walked on a street or got out of my car wherever, I would see coins strewn around and have to pick them up. Around my house, coins were everywhere – on the floor, on counters, on tables, in corners and under furniture. I had not left coins in those places. Then came the day when I vacuumed under the heavy living room chair he had sat in a lot. I knew there was no coin left there. For some reason, I was compelled to move the chair the next day. There was a dime in the middle spot under that chair.

I had coins in my car and in my pockets. I bought a cheap sculptured wishing well and started putting all the found coins into the pail and the well. It began to fill up.

My found coins are in the wishing well. I cannot spend them. I just need to keep the coins as a reminder of being reminded that there is unseen energy that manifests or creates and moves coins.

Just another Story

HORSES

my first horse

Horses have the final word. Horses have somehow been in my life at major crossroads. While nearing the end of writing this book, horses began to show up in my visions and dreams. It is as though they want recognition. They would stop by and look me in the face, or they would run by in a way that I would notice. I recognize some as horses I have known but are long gone. On the other hand, they are not gone considering their soul energy is alive and making an impact on this book. It is as though they are saying, "Hey, we've been with you whenever you wanted us in your life, so don't leave us out now at this milestone."

I have an uncanny audio and visual memory that goes back to babyhood, so I remember my introduction to horses. When visiting my grandparents' farm, my father would sit me on the back his horse named Tony as soon as I could sit. He would lead me around the farmyard of his childhood. Riding on his horse became a safe haven where I felt completely at peace in the world, safe from harm in the gentle protection of a horse that understood me as a tiny human being. Wherever I went throughout the day, Tony's eyes would follow me with special caring. Over the next five years, four more children were born and lined up around me on Tony's back.

Tony and my father unleashed their wild side in an otherwise leashed in and responsible way of life that each had when separate. My father had work in the city and had to leave Tony on the farm. On each visit to the farm when there was no snow, they would race across the pastures and over the hills, then come back breathless but knowing they had protected each other in their shared love of wind and speed. I was like my exuberant, high-spirited father in many ways. As the oldest child, I always got the best of him. My father always raced Tony bareback and that became my preferred way to ride horses.

Riding bareback meant the horse and I became one; I could feel his energy and muscles and I responded with mine. Our energy blended.

I was quite grown up when my grandparents came to the city for a visit and delivered bad news to my father. When he asked about his Tony, they said Tony had been sold because he was old.

I had never seen my father cry until that day. He cried for days and weeks. His grief was heart wrenching.

As a young girl, I had been present when a male calf was loaded onto a truck. My heart broke. I watched the sadness in his eyes watching me as he was driven away down the dirt road until he disappeared. I will never forget him as long as I am alive. Even now, I can see his eyes. I made the decision that day that I would never marry a farmer and face decisions of raising and killing animals for food or for any other reason.

My grandparents were gentle and kind people but they were farmers. I could not understand why on earth my father's horse had not been allowed to die a natural death in the pastures of his home? I would never come to peace about this.

At mid-summer exhibition time, my father went by himself to make a beeline to the racehorses. He was not there to bet. He came home claiming that his Tony was there, running races and that he had been able to spend a few minutes in the barn talking to him.

I will never know if my father was pacifying himself or me with hopeful thinking, or if Tony had defied death by getting recognized for his love of racing.

sisters go riding

In early teen years, my sister and I went to the barn where two giant workhorses were in their stalls. We decided to go for a ride. With the help of the stall sidewalls, we mounted the back of the horses without bridles or saddles. The horses backed out of their stalls and walked toward the open doors and out. On wide, brown backs of muscle, we held onto their heavy mains and headed for pasture. We relied on words, subtle touching beside the horses' necks and our heels that dug into their sides to give directions. These well-trained workhorses responded, taking direction for a while.

These horses were used to pull heavy things like plows, wagons, and sleighs in winter. They had never had a rider before this day. In the middle of the pasture, a long way from the farmyard, my sister's horse decided he would shake his rider off his back. He sidestepped in one direction, and then quickly changed his direction. My sister fell off. It was a long way to the ground where she lay. The horse seemed to take pity as he stood beside her and watched for whatever was to come.

My sister lay on her back on the ground, looking at the sky, saying, "I'm dead! I'm dead!"

I was still high above her on my horse that also stopped to watch. I looked down – way down – and was overtaken with the comedy. My sister was quite alive! I burst into roaring laughter so hard that my sister got up in disgust and started walking back home. In that moment, somehow the comedy kept us from even thinking of possible injuries. My sister had fallen from a great height and did not get hurt. Her horse hung his head low and followed on her heels. It was as though the giant was sorry and at least could make it up by protecting the young girl all the way home. He even followed her right into the barn.

When we entered the barn, my sister showed her horse to his stall. He obeyed. Meanwhile, I had to dismount my horse. Somehow, I managed to slip down but ended up behind my horse. He stepped back; his hind right foot landed on my foot.

I was pinned to the concrete floor with a ton of weight on top of my foot. I hurt so much that I was silenced. I could not even yell. In my pain, I was sure I was being paid back for laughing at my sister. I looked up, wondering how to move the weight and I realized the immense height and width of the behind of this horse. His tail was way above my head. I was looking at a wall of unmovable brown horse rear end. After what seemed like an eternity, my horse moved his foot. In some kind of miracle, I was also fine, not even a limp.

We were two resilient girls playing with powerful forces and came out unscathed, just hoping no adults would find out what we had done. And somehow, two horses had used their power to look after two courageous but silly girls.

I still burst into laughter just for remembering and writing this story, and again and again in editing.

fourteen years old

Horses played a major role in charting my life when I was aged fourteen. My girlfriend and I shared a love of riding horses. All week we saved our babysitting money and did everything possible to slip away on Sunday mornings. We took the Greyhound bus to Regina Beach and walked from there to the farm that rented riding horses.

My girlfriend came up with the idea that we could train for a career as jockeys. I had no career plans at the moment; I knew more about what I did not want to do. I knew that being a farmer's wife was at the top of my list as a not-for-me. I had failed to become a concert pianist like my mother would have liked; my excuse was that I had no piano to practice on. I had and did not appreciate an old parlor organ with heavy foot pedals and a too short keyboard. I did not want to be a nurse, teacher or the wife of a hockey player or a red coated Mounted policeman, as many prairie girls I knew aspired to be. Training to be a jockey sounded good right then.

We always asked for light English riding saddles. We would ride away from prying eyes and stop to set the stirrups high. Then we would race, practicing to be jockeys. With our horses, we abandoned all life's concerns and experienced pure happiness as we raced each other around pastures, sometime through bush, and if one of us got knocked off by a tree branch, we would just get back on. We were fearless. We had no riding boots, so our ankles were worn through to the bones and bled but we were happy all week until we could do it again the following Sunday.

We always had to walk our horses after riding because they foamed with heat and the owners were not pleased. But every Sunday, they rented horses to us again regardless that they knew what we did.

My father was suspicious that I may be disappearing each Sunday to meet a boy. I tried to convince him that we only met horses. So one Sunday he drove us to the supposed horses and was surprised that our story was true. He never bothered me again about meeting boys on Sunday.

As fate would have it, the very next Sunday after my father's visit to the farm, I did meet a young man at the horses and that meeting would be the fork in the road for me. To that day, I had never so much as kissed a boy. I was still fourteen and innocent as could possibly be, and ready for trouble now that my dad was no longer worried about me.

My girlfriend and I had just finished walking our horses to cool them down and headed back to the barn. There he stood – a guy dressed like Cisco Kid. He was entirely different than any boy I had ever seen. He sure was not a farm boy or like any guys at school. He was eighteen and a new immigrant from Germany looking like he had just stepped out of a movie.

He immediately became interested in me. We talked and when I found out he was hungry, I walked clear into town to find a woman I knew to be at the beach, who still owed me money for babysitting. Oddly, I met her and her baby right away on the main street. With the money, I headed straight for the fish and chips stand. I walked back to the farm with the food. He was still there waiting for me. We sat in the tall grass by a fence while he ate.

Feeding him was obviously the key to his heart. From then on, he was at the farm waiting for me every Sunday. He joined my girlfriend and me for rides but our wild racing was slowed and soon stopped. By the end of the summer he managed to ride with me while she rode somewhere nearby. For the last ride of the season, his choice was to have me ride on one horse with him. We abandoned a saddle and he insisted I sit in front of him. Out in the field, far from any prying eyes, he managed to slip his hands under my clothes. While I sat on the back of a horse, I felt the sensation of a man's hands for the first time in my life.

At age fourteen, I had a choice to make. Could I – would I give in to long years of curiosity and daydreams about the wonders of sex? We were a long way out on the prairie that lay flat for miles under the clear blue sky with only a few small, fluffy white clouds floating by to hear me or see me. If I got off the horse, I would be alone with him in that vast prairie land. My small body would be no match in a wrestling match with this man. I was riding in front and had the reigns in my hands. I circled the horse to head back to the barn, which my horse was happy to do and picked up to an easy, smooth trot. So, as the explorer dreamily explored my body, he lost his attention on direction. He came to a sudden realization that the barn was in front of us and the farmer was watching us approach. This horse brought me to sudden safety where I found my freedom of a different kind.

The wildly exhilarating summer of racing horses with my girlfriend was over for that year. A new and jarring experience had happened to me. It had been a summer to remember.

my little boy

Years later, I found a new riding partner. He was a bachelor living on the neighboring farm to my brother's farm. This man and I had a horsy friendship that served his loneliness and my love of horses. He had a muscled black stallion that looked like a poster horse and he was a rough cowboy kind of rider. He also had a gentler brown mare and offered her to me on my summer holidays. I would leave my family to whatever they were doing and go riding with him every afternoon. He had passion for riding through rough terrain. We would find our way through dense bush, over rocks and mud, and follow creeks. For me, this was a new experience and I enjoyed every minute while watching for my horse's footwork to keep her safe.

Again, my father watched and was not happy that I was going riding instead of behaving as he thought a married woman should. So one day, as I was ready to go riding, he told me to pick and can peas from the garden. I went to the pea patch and looked at the peas drying on the vine. I had a horse waiting for me and a neighbor waited who wanted to ride with me. There was no contest between peas and horses. I took off through the crop of oats to where the neighbor and his horses waited.

For the second time since I was a young girl, my father who understood loving horses, gave up and let me be. He never brought it up again. Riding had come back into my life and I was feeling a happy freedom that had only to do with riding a horse. Nothing else compared.

Then came the day when I had my mare tied up overnight to a fence only a few feet from my brother's house and close to where I slept in our parked van. I had no idea my mare was ready for breeding that night. My brother's horses took advantage of her being tied up and unable to run away.

When the foal was born, he was a beautiful brown little boy with a white star on his forehead. My riding friend decided the foal should be mine. He put him and his mother on my brother's farm for when I would return to claim ownership. I did come back the next summer and managed to take pictures of my little guy nursing on his mother. I named him Star. But – I was also going through a divorce. This would be my last visit to the farm for years to come.

Meanwhile, the neighbor took back his gift and sold him at auction. I could only hope and pray that he found a good home. I would never know what happened to my little boy – where he ended up.

His picture reminds me of how innocent horses are unable to defend themselves against the whims of humans who decide their fate. His picture also reminds me of the magical life that I experienced with my horses.

the guardian

Rocky stood there beside the fence, watching us. He caught my eye. He was a forlorn horse that had been treated badly on a farm where we went to buy hay. I knew I could not leave him behind and was thrilled to hear he was for sale. So I rode him for a few minutes. I could feel his gentle soul. I had no way to keep him so I bought him as a gift.

This horse was of mixed breed and physically he was not as sleek and exotic as those purebred horses he would share pasture with, and he was shy of men because of harsh training. To get to know him, the new owner allowed him space. They would look at each other across space. Each day, the space between them would get smaller and soon they were whispering to each other. Then came the day when he became the favorite riding companion. He had a good, protected, gentle life for the next few years.

There came the day when a toddler went missing. It is unusual for a horse to lay down with a person but when found, the toddler was asleep in the barn with Rocky lying beside him in full protection.

dogs and cats

Now that the horse stories are being told, I am getting reminders that dogs and cats want to be told.

I have always had animals in my life. Animals are unconditional love if treated right. They are completely loyal and will stay close to their loved ones no matter what the situation. Because of that loyalty, the dogs and cats that I have known in life and are now dead continue to surround me. In other words, I have a lot of animals in my life – living ones and some are in spirit form.

Often I am aware that my bed is shared with those who have passed. I feel jumping onto my bed. I look and nothing is there. Then I feel the nestling in around my feet.

When we bought the house I live in now, there was a grey cat that many family members would see. The cat was seen to run around the house, then toward the balcony and disappear into the air. The invisible cat would sit by my head when I went to bed. I would fall asleep with purring. Because so many people would see the cat, we all knew him to be real but in spirit.

My tiny Maltipoo had survived three cancer operations, but on a day this year when she was happy and healthy she died of a heart attack out of fear while in a veterinary clinic for a checkup. It was extremely unexpected. I was in shock for weeks and suffered terrible guilt. She believed I was her protector! She had come to me from a puppy mill on a Saskatchewan farm. She fit into the palm of my hand but she had to hoard food to survive. She was frightened and I could not touch her hind end. On first contact with me, she glued herself to my chest and that's where she stayed for months inside a scarf. Now, she came to me in spirit in a lucid dream. In life, she was a deep thinker and always checked my face and eyes to read what I was thinking and feeling. She did that in my dream. She looked deep into my eyes right to my soul. She wanted me to know she continues to be with me.

At night, in order for her to identify herself from my larger dog who passed on years earlier and continues to be in my bed, she would tug at blankets that hung close to the floor. In life, she was not large enough to jump onto the bed. I would put out my hand, as I would have in life to lift her onto the bed. Then she would settle in around me. Her way of identifying herself, reminds me of the keen intelligence of animals.

What we all need to know is that animals do continue caring for us.

I grew up with a story as told by my mother. My mother and her brother and sister were children when their mother died of a hospital borne infection three days after giving birth. This death was a shock to everyone because all her other births had been at home; this birth in hospital was a gift that took her life. At night, after their mother died, the children would be aware that a small white dog would visit each of them and watch over them all night long.

The family did not own a dog. The children had a guardian angel in the form of a small white dog.

The question I have always had is whether or not the small dog was their mother's spirit taking on the look of a small dog that would not frighten the small children, or was the dog a dog guardian spirit?

under the sleigh

It was a whiteout. Snow was piling high in the prairie blizzard. My aunt was nine months pregnant and hoping what she was feeling was only false labor, just a preparation for the real thing in a few days.

She did not want to give birth in the farmhouse on the vast white prairie where even neighbors were miles apart, and there were no modern conveniences. She wanted all the help she could get in a hospital.

My uncle's attitude was not to be concerned because they both were from farmer families. They had seen a lot of animals giving birth, and besides, he had returned from being a soldier in World War II not very long ago and he was quite used to roughing it. He told my aunt he could figure it out when the time came.

Within a few hours, it seemed the time had come. She looked out the window at the weather and insisted they go to the hospital.

He was not about to argue with a woman experiencing contractions that were comparable to no pain he ever knew. He felt humbled with each contraction.

They would still have a few hours of daylight for the trip. The blizzard had given way to glistening soft snowfall. The wind had subsided.

The country dirt roads were impassible by car. My uncle dusted snow off the sleigh. The sleigh, he figured, would be comfortable enough because it was large and had proper seats and railings. He teamed up two workhorses and hitched them to the sleigh. It might take a couple of hours to get to the hospital through the snow, but he was convinced that if she bundled into enough blankets, they should be able to make it just fine.

The first hour was a continuation of the kind of contractions that she had been having.

Then suddenly, she felt the need to push. She tried to stay calm and not push with each contraction. She tried to hold back what was happening.

With a yell that carried far, she told him the baby was coming.

It was cold and still snowing.

My uncle halted the horses. He turned to his wife and suggested that they turn the sleigh over and make a bed under the sleigh. He helped her out of the sleigh. With the help of his horses, he managed to flip the heavy sleigh over in a hurry.

He unhitched the horses so that they would not accidentally move the sleigh. Now they were free to wander away if they wanted to, but he would face that hurdle when he had to.

He made a bed under the sleigh where my aunt continued hard contractions that kept her body heated regardless of the cold temperature outside. She found the bed quite comfortable on top of soft snow. Very soon, a healthy boy gave a lusty cry. My uncle had no way to cut the cord, so baby and placenta were placed onto the mother's bare chest under her clothing. In midwifery, this is called the kangaroo protection of baby and is most desired.

As though guardians of the birth, the horses had been standing close and silent. Their first sounds were a few snorts, heavy breathing and the stamping of a couple of hooves when they heard the baby cry. The horses sounded relieved.

Then it was time to go the rest of the way through the snow to the hospital. Mother and baby were in good shape after the birth under the sleigh.

roundup

I would ride again at another change in the map of my life. In week two of a new relationship, the new man and I decided to visit my sister and her husband at their ranch. We had a nice evening conversation and slept there. Waking up to breakfast on the ranch, I discovered this was a day for rounding up hundreds of cows and calves in preparation to take them to greener pastures in the Foothills of Alberta's Rocky Mountains. Of course, I was excited and offered to help.

My brother-in-law was a tough, older rancher and rodeo rider always in saddle. In getting our horses ready for riding, I took a bridle but refused to have a saddle. He was surprised and at first amused, but he let me have my way. His amusement peaked as he worked the roundup at one side while watching me do as perfect a job as he was doing while I was riding bareback at the opposite side. I was doing what he had never seen before in my agility to ride bareback and make quick turns and twists to round up my runaways and get them all channeled into a corral without any help.

Meanwhile, the new man in my life was watching from a fence. He was to see an unexpected side of me. What a surprise! I had never seen such delightful amazement and appreciation all at once in a man's face.

When finished rounding up cattle, my horse walked me over to him. He asked to ride with me. With the help of the fence, he mounted behind me. He clung tightly to my waist. This was the beginning of a very long relationship. We rode away as he whispered wonderful words into my neck.

☆〇

about back cover painting

Horses have always been in my life one way or another, marking many milestones. The back cover painting on this book depicts the freeing, wild side of releasing these stories.

H.T.A. Heisler

Love never ends

www.ingramcontent.com/pod-product-compliance
Lightning Source LLC
Chambersburg PA
CBHW060743050426
42449CB00008B/1299